from Freeborn
to Freetown & Back

Patrick O'Leary in Binkolo, Sierra Leone, in 1968.
Photo taken by Kathleen Nardina.

from Freeborn
to Freetown & Back

Patrick R. O'Leary

A PEACE CORPS WRITERS BOOK

FROM FREEBORN TO FREETOWN AND BACK

A Peace Corps Writers Book
An imprint of Peace Corps Worldwide

Printed in the United States of America
by Peace Corps Writers of Oakland, California.

For more information, contact peacecorpsworldwide@gmail.com.

Peace Corps Writers and the Peace Corps Writers colophon are trademarks of PeaceCorpsWorldwide.org

Cover photos: O'Leary family farmhouse, Freeborn County, Minnesota (2007), by Patrick O'Leary. Camel Back rock formation near Binkolo, Sierra Leone (2012), by Peter C. Andersen. Garra cloth from Makeni, Sierra Leone, and author's last pair of "Peace Corps sandals," from 1968 (2016), by Patrick O'Leary. Author photo by Elizabeth Striegler.

ISBN-13: 978-1-935925-78-1

Library of Congress Control Number: 2016943946

First Peace Corps Writers Edition, September 2016

20   19   18   17   16   1   2   3   4   5   6   7   8   9   10

*These stories are dedicated
to the idea that encourages us to leave home
and family to explore and to expand our comfort zones
to include environments and people who may look,
believe, live, and speak in ways that are not familiar to us.
This pursuit expands the learning of those of us who dare
as well as those we meet.*

I want to believe my experience was beneficial for many.

*Hearing and responding to different drums
can be wonderful!*

Contents

Author's Note

The stories in this book are based primarily on memories of things that happened years ago. My memory has faded, of course, and it can be selective as well—vulnerable to exaggeration and fabrication. For example, when I visited Makeni in 2004, I was convinced that what had once been the Makeni Peace Corps Rest House was now a bare foundation of corn stalks with an abandoned auto rusting away. I got a jolt a couple of years later when my former Peace Corps supervisor sent me a photo he had taken sometime in 2006 of the still-habitable former rest house.

Fortunately, I serendipitously kept the letter that provides the institutional record of my service in Sierra Leone, which was written by Joseph C. Kennedy, Peace Corps Director in Sierra Leone. Readers can use their own judgment to assess any discrepancies between the official description of my service and what I have described here.

~ ~ ~

PEACE CORPS
Washington, D.C. 20525

Mr. Patrick R. O'Leary entered training on October 10, 1966 at Syracuse University, New York and on December 20, 1966 completed an intensive ten-week program. Included in the subjects studied were methods of teaching, practice teaching, teaching English as a Second Language and intensive Swahili language and Tanzania area studies. However, after training, the Tanzania program was cancelled and Mr. O'Leary was assigned to an agricultural position in Sierra Leone for which he had nine weeks training in-country concentrating on Agriculture and construction.

He was enrolled as a Peace Corps Volunteer on December 20, 1966. Upon arrival in Sierra Leone he was assigned to Binkolo, Safroko-Limba Chiefdom as a Chiefdom Development worker and was responsible to the Ministry of Interior and the District Officer. His work consisted mainly of agricultural extension, seed rice distribution, distribution and proper application of chemical fertilizers and improved varieties of vegetables.

Additionally, during Mr. O'Leary's final three months, he worked at St. Augustine Teacher Training College, Makeni, supervising laborers in various construction projects on the college campus.

. . .

December 1, 1968   Joseph C. Kennedy
                                                        Peace Corps Director
                                                        Sierra Leone

1.

Leaving Freeborn County

The 1966 annual Knights of Columbus summer picnic was held at Helmer Myre State Park (now Myre–Big Island State Park), near Albert Lea, in Freeborn County, Minnesota. Many of the people who attended knew I would soon be leaving for Peace Corps training and that I would be going to Africa.

A woman I had known my whole life approached me. She had been my mother's nurse when I was born twenty-two years earlier. I had served Mass at her father's funeral. Our school choir had sung at the High Mass when she and a local banker married in 1958.

"Pat, I hear you are going to Africa."

"Yes, I hope so, but I don't know where yet."

"Have a wonderful time, but don't bring one back."

I was stunned by her bluntness. But her remark was similar to others, made around the same time, by a fellow who had been my classmate for sixteen years—my best friend in first grade. I had purchased a pair of oxblood penny loafers at an August "Crazy Days Sale" on Broadway Avenue in Albert Lea, and when my friend saw me wearing them he said, "Pat. Why did you buy those nigger shoes?" I bought them because they were different, they fit, they were a good deal. I was befuddled by the comment and could not understand where it came from.

A few weeks later I was invited to become a member of Tanzania XIII.

2.

Where I Started From

In August of 1966 I had a summer job with the Freeborn County Highway Department. I was working with the seal coating crew on County Road 29, between MN Highway 13 and Freeborn, Minnesota, when my dad, the foreman for the county highway department, drove up one afternoon and gave me a large envelope that had been delivered to our home mailbox. It was from the United States Peace Corps. I had been accepted to Tanzania XIII. I had requested duty in Tanzania because I had become interested in it during geography classes sometime in my earlier schooling.

Before I opened that envelope I had rarely been far from Freeborn County. I had been in Iowa, which was just a few miles south of my home, once or twice. I had never been more than 30 miles west of where I stood. I had been to a Dominican monastery in Dubuque, Iowa, for a weekend retreat during my senior year of college. I had twice been to St. Louis, Missouri, to visit my sister, Geraldine, a Maryknoll novitiate nun. I had been to Minneapolis/St. Paul for two University of Minnesota football games, and once for a Minnesota Intercollegiate Athletic Conference volleyball tournament at Hamline

University in St. Paul. My only extraordinary excursion had been to
Key West, Florida, over the 1964 Christmas holidays with two seminary classmates, Tom Wegman and Norman Wieseler, and Mike Ahl,
a cousin of Wegman's.

That trip was an adventure and a blur. We drove straight through
from Rochester, Minnesota, to Miami and then to Key West in Wegman's black 1952 Cadillac hearse, which he had bought for $250. A
driver and a passenger rode in the front seats, and two others rode in
back, resting or sleeping on a large foam-rubber mattress. We stopped
once to patch a tire in Birmingham, Alabama. As the tire was being
repaired, a local fellow noticed the open back door of the hearse and
asked, "Are you using that mattress for immoral purpose?" I was
amused by his demeanor and language, and wondered what he was
talking about.

~   ~   ~

I was raised on a short leash. Until I was five years old my father
worked five days a week as a ditch digger and tiler for the Freeborn
County Highway Department, and evenings as a time keeper for the
Wilson and Company Meat Packing House in Albert Lea. When he
was promoted to foreman at the highway department, he quit the job
at Wilson's and purchased a rundown 98-acre farmstead 5 miles north
of Albert Lea. Rundown meant: a house with electricity and running
water, an outhouse, an abandoned barn and silo, a granary, and two
other out buildings. On May 1, 1951, when I was soon to be seven
years old, we moved to the farm. My mother gave birth to my brother
Daniel on May 28. For the next eleven years I labored: working with
Dad tearing down buildings; digging ditches; hauling chicken, cow,
and pig manure in a Sears and Roebuck garden wheelbarrow; cutting
down box elder trees with a two-man crosscut saw to heat the house;
digging out tree stumps; milking cows; butchering chickens; building
fences; and helping to make our farm a sacred place for what eventually
became a home for my parents and their eleven children.

Shortly after we moved to the farm, one of the out buildings
became a garage. A forced-air furnace had been installed in the base-

ment before we moved into the house. For the first two years our fuel was coal; later, wood—until 1988, when my dad had a heart attack and could no longer cut wood.

For a few of my years on the farm we sold eggs from the chickens we raised. The egg money became grocery money at the nearby Bancroft store.

We later raised three hundred chicken roosters for meat. As the chicks matured and became butcher size, it was common for ten or twelve of them to be caged in the yard on Friday nights so they would empty their gizzards and bowels, which would make it easier to kill and gut them in preparation for later meals. I often thought Dad started butchering the chickens earlier than I would have, but with the number of mouths to feed, his hurry to butcher is likely understandable. We ate well.

Our first manure spreader consisted of me and the Sears and Roebuck garden wheelbarrow, which I used until its wheel bearing wore out. I was excited and relieved when Dad acquired a construction-type wheelbarrow with a larger box and a rubber tire to replace it. A later manure spreader, in disrepair but tractor pulled, was so broken that I had to use a pitchfork to throw manure on to the spreader and later off into the fields.

Dad and I spent one Memorial Day weekend digging and tiling a ditch through our driveway, by hand, to drain a wet area on one side. We later dug tile lines under the township road to connect and drain fields on the south side of the property. It was a lot of work, and not unusual to dig until dark on many summer evenings.

Albert Lea, 5 miles way, barely registered in my world then. For me, Albert Lea meant church, parochial school, the public library, and relatives. My relatives were mostly laborers, farmers, horsemen, and maybe wayward drinkers. We were Irish but mostly not sophisticated enough to be "lace curtain Irish" or sensitive to what was to become a Celtic renaissance of sorts in the later twentieth century. I was dimly aware that there were such things as Belleek porcelain and Waterford crystal. With my mother often pregnant, much of my time away from the farm focused on visiting extended family and trips to rural cemeteries in Bath, Newry, and Twin Lakes, all in Freeborn County, where many relatives were buried. Before my high school graduation I hadn't been far from the farm except for imaginary travel through books and especially AM radio, listening to major league baseball games and a lot of rock and roll and rhythm and blues from stations in Del Rio, Nashville, Shreveport, Little Rock, Chicago, Detroit, and New York City.

When I was fourteen, an Albert Lea priest drove us eighth- and ninth-grade altar boys to nearby Rochester to tour the Mother House of the Third Order of St. Francis nuns, some of whom staffed the Albert Lea parochial schools. We also visited St. Mary's College in Winona. That was when I crossed the Mississippi River for the first time.

As we rode through Rochester I saw my first skyscraper—part of the Mayo Clinic. It was twenty stories tall, and attached to one side was a large nude sculpture. This was a big deal to me. I had never seen such a thing; I knew I was in a sophisticated place.

During our time in Rochester many of the altar boys bought peas and peashooters at the Miracle Mile Shopping Center not far from St. Mary's Hospital, and they had peashooter fights on the bus most of the way back to Albert Lea. The young priest did not have enough presence of mind to simply stop the bus and grab all the peashooters from the guys. We were fortunate no one was hit in the eye. We had a great time.

~ ~ ~

I entered first grade at Albert Lea's St. Theodore grade school in 1950 and attended parochial school for nine years. I might have gone to the nearby public country school, but my parents were strong advocates and supporters of Catholic education and wanted me to go to the Catholic school. But there would be a cost for me to ride the public school bus to and from the parochial school. My parents seemed anguished over their decision. I do not know if the anguish was due to the cost or to the thought of a Catholic kid riding a public school bus.

I was apprehensive about leaving home and starting school. With my dad then working two jobs, I had largely been around my mother, my relatives, and my mother's coffee/birthday club neighbors. I felt awkward riding with big kids on the bus. When I was riding home on one of the first school days, an older public school girl beckoned to me and handed me a green Wrigley's Spearmint gum wrapper. I was excited and pleased to have a gift from a new friend. I opened the gift. There was no gum. A public school kid had stiffed me. I thought I had been stiffed because I was Catholic.

We moved to the farm a year later. School buses were still not available to pick up parochial school students. We rode to town with Dad as he drove to work. He dropped us off at the church and school at about 7:15 AM and picked us up shortly after 5:00 PM. This was the routine for my siblings and me for at least ten years. Except when we visited Albert Lea's Carnegie Public Library after school, we were usually on the St. Theodore's church and school grounds. During my senior year in high school, I was the janitor at St. Theodore's grade school. By then there were usually four or five of my siblings somewhere around the grounds; we were together a lot.

~   ~   ~

My first experience with Albert Lea's public school system was not positive. It was a four-week summer school world history class at the high school in 1959. Twenty to twenty-five students were in the class; four of us parochial school classmates, freshmen, were attending public school for the first time. There were no outstanding concerns in the class until our studies reached the Reformation period and the teacher, Mr. Johnson, seemed to spend most of one week baiting us four Catholic students about the Catholic Church, Martin Luther, and so on.

During the following school year, Mr. Johnson, also a track coach, stopped me in the hall and encouraged me to come out for the track team. I had run a good time in a physical education class. But with my school work, farm work, and only one car in the family, participation in track would have been difficult. I would have had to run the five or so miles to and from home and somehow manage to attend track meets. But Mr. Johnson had soured me so much with his summer school behavior that I did not try to pursue the issue with him.

Another event at the public high school that left a sour taste in my mouth occurred when an aging male violinist performed at a school assembly. I was a junior or senior. Some of the students in the audience did not appreciate his playing. Some began to jeer and hurl pennies at him. He stopped performing, berated the audience, and began to list performances he had given around the world. This did not move many in the audience in a positive way. I thought the students' behavior was humiliating and that it reflected upon the public school.

~   ~   ~

Albert Lea did not seem like a particularly friendly place in other ways, too. There seemed to be prejudice and fear in many, though over time I didn't know or understand what they had to fear. There were a few Hispanic residents—and a few more Hispanic migrant workers in vegetable fields near Hollandale during the summer—but otherwise Freeborn County's population was white except for a small Native American group, seemingly from somewhere in Nebraska. One of them, "the Chief," worked with Dad at the county and helped pour cement with us for the building that became our barn. My parents' prejudices seemed to be primarily scars from having lived in compact interrelated rural Irish Catholic communities that were breaking down as members of the community intermingled and intermarried with Danes, Norwegians, Germans, Dutch, Czechs, Bohemians, Hispanics, Lutherans, Baptists, and others who populated the county.

3.

What Got Me
to Want to Explore

As the oldest of eleven children on a farm, I had a lot of work to do and not a lot of free time for activities other than reading, taking care of siblings, and babysitting neighbor kids. Bonnie Callahan, a schoolteacher aunt of my mother, gave us a copy of the book *I Married Adventure*, Osa Johnson's memoir of living and traveling with her husband, Martin Johnson, a documentary filmmaker, in parts of East and Central Africa, the islands of the South Pacific, and British North Borneo from 1917 to 1936. Whatever I understood of what was in the book I'm not sure, but I became captivated with East Africa and Africa in general, and I thought I wanted to go there. When I filled out my Peace Corps application, sometime in my senior year in college, I indicated I wished to go to Tanganyika, renamed Tanzania in 1965.

I was also motivated by the Peace Corps idea, originally sketched and proposed by Hubert H. Humphrey in 1957 and later picked up by John F. Kennedy during his presidential campaign in a speech at the University of Michigan on October 14, 1960. An additional motivation was Vince McCauley, an uncle of my father, who was involved in the Middle East as part of George Patton's army during the Second

World War. I had met Vince only once in my young life, but my dad's face and eyes lit up whenever Vince's name was mentioned. Whatever Vince had been doing seemed inspiring and exotic to some in our family, including me. The Peace Corps seemed like a good way to travel, to explore, and to see a different world with a very different group of people than those to whom I was accustomed.

~   ~   ~

For my first three years at St. Mary's College in Winona, Minnesota, I was a member of a class of more than ninety students at Immaculate Heart of Mary Seminary. This was the first group of guys I had ever been with who seemed to think I could be a fine fellow. After my third year, the seminary faculty was apparently perceptive enough of my attitudes and behavior to believe I was moving in a direction other than a commitment to the priesthood. I was really seeking a means of getting away from all I had known, and to be part of things I did not know.

I applied to the Peace Corps early in my senior year St. Mary's. During that year the only indication I might still be on track for this journey was when Monsignor Joseph R. McGinnis, rector of Immaculate Heart of Mary Seminary, approached me while I was at an intermural softball game and told me he had been contacted by the Peace Corps and wished me good fortune. Later that summer, George Murphy, the Assistant Freeborn County Engineer, a relative and supervisor of the engineering survey crew I worked with for two years, told my parents he had also been contacted. George told my mother his answer to the question "Does Pat have a sense of humor?" was "Yes. If you can find it."

4.

Tanzania XIII

My first airplane ride, in October 1966, was from Rochester, Minnesota, to Syracuse, New York. I was excited to be on my way to somewhere. I flew American Airlines and found the steak sandwich dinner served during the flight magnificent! I can still taste it so many years later.

Tanzania XIII, the thirteenth Peace Corps program for trainees going to Tanzania, was held at the School of East African Studies, Syracuse University, Syracuse, New York. It trained people to become primary and secondary school teachers in Tanzania, teachers for a Dar es Salaam law school, and commercial instructors for a business school. We were to be in training for ten weeks. Upon completion of training, if successful and not "de-selected," we would be sent to Tanzania.

One hundred and seventy of us were housed in two-bedroom apartments, which had functioned as married students' housing near the campus. I lived with four men; two were Jewish, one was a Baptist Bible banger from New Jersey, and one was an Irish guy who had graduated from Notre Dame in law. I was meeting people from all over the country. Everyone was different; even the music we listened to was different. I was in a new country! I was becoming someone else.

Training began on October 10, 1966. It consisted of seminars and classes on Tanzanian culture, language, history, economics, and so forth. We took part in a course called "Teaching English as a Second Language," plus Swahili classes three hours a day, six days a week, taught by East African graduate students from Kenya, Uganda, and Tanzania.

We also had cross-cultural experiences that enabled Peace Corps staff to observe how we reacted to new environments. Each of us spent a week in one of three places: sea islands near the coast of Georgia; somewhere near Brattleboro, Vermont; and Horse Creek, Kentucky, not far from Manchester in Laurel County. I was sent to Horse Creek.

In Horse Creek I lived in the home of a woman named Granny Wilkins. I "insulated" her house by nailing cardboard to its inside walls. All of us worked with the recently started local Community Action Program. One of our tasks was to seek signatures for petitions to have running water piped into private homes in the "hollers." At the time, many residents' primary source of water was polluted runoff from local coal mines. Beyond these very practical and important tasks, I have a memory, real or imagined, of attending an evening church service with ministers who used poisonous snakes during one of the services. And at least once during my stay there I had a sip of "white lighting" (moonshine).

After returning to Syracuse, I spent time practice-teaching fifth grade in the Syracuse public school system. I was not a success. I was in danger of being de-selected. But Peace Corps staff knew of my farming background, and I was asked to write about it. I did. My writing and a later interview with staff enabled me to remain in the program.

When we completed our training, we celebrated with a banquet a week or so before Christmas. At the dinner the Tanzania XIII training director, Gary Gappert, stood at the dais and said, "Congratulations! You are going to Africa! However, the Tanzanian government doesn't want some of you to come. You will be sent somewhere else. Go home for the holidays. You will hear from us!"

Julius Nyerere, the President of Tanzania, was advocating a program known as "Uhuru na Ujumaa" (Self-Help and Self-Direction) for the country. He canceled the Tanzania XIII program. He may have believed that too many expatriates were coming to the country and disrupting its life; he may have believed something else. Years later a Tanzanian woman, a St. Paul neighbor of mine, told me Nyerere's decision may have been based in part on opposition to US government policy on Israel and/or Vietnam.

I returned to Minnesota for the 1966 Christmas holidays. In early January I received notice that I would be sent to Sierra Leone. I somehow knew it had been called "the Athens of West Africa," but I didn't know why. It had also been known as "the White Man's Grave." I visited the Albert Lea library to learn what I could about the country, but it had very little information.

I eventually learned that Europe and North America have a long and significant history of mutual involvement with Sierra Leone. The first Europeans to encounter what is now known as Sierra Leone were Portuguese sailors seeking a route to the New World. Many of the first Africans who were taken to North America and enslaved were brought from Sierra Leone to the sea islands off the coasts of Georgia and South Carolina to grow rice. The 1997 Steven Spielberg film *Amistad*, a story of revolt on a slave ship coming to America in 1839, featured a number of characters from parts of West Africa now known as Sierra Leone.

In 1787 British philanthropists founded the Sierra Leone Colony on the Sierra Leone peninsula. It was ruled by the British Sierra Leone Company. That same year a group they called the "Black Poor"—former American slaves who had been servicemen of the British Crown during the American War of Independence—was sent to Sierra Leone after first having been sent to Nova Scotia. Some of the Black Poor came directly from London. In 1800 the "Maroons," former slaves who had revolted against the British in Jamaica, were also sent to Nova Scotia and later to Sierra Leone. Another group, the "Recaptives," were Africans captured on slave ships on the way to North America and taken to Freetown. Between 1808 and roughly 1850 about fifty thousand Recaptives were brought to Freetown.

In the early nineteenth century, Freetown served as the seat of the British colonial government in West Africa. Sierra Leone also served as the educational center of British West Africa. I eventually learned that "the Athens of West Africa" was a name for Freetown's Forah Bay College, the first and oldest Western-style college in sub-Saharan Africa, founded in 1827. The college was required to maintain British standards of excellence in order to be recognized as providing a university education. The school eventually attracted students from many parts of West Africa.

"The White Man's Grave" was a name given to Sierra Leone Colony, Britain's first in West Africa, established in 1807. The name came from the fate of many whites and former slaves who went there to preach, to rule, and to live, but instead died of malaria, yellow fever, and other maladies.

~   ~   ~

When I received notice that I would be going to Sierra Leone, I requested that the Peace Corps arrange to fly me from Rochester to Sierra Leone. I was instead informed that I was to fly from Fairmont, Minnesota, to Minneapolis to New York, and then to West Africa. I received no such a ticket and petitioned for a second itinerary. I eventually received a ticket to leave from Minneapolis. One January day, in the midst of a storm that left eight inches of snow on the ground, Dad drove me to Albert Lea's train depot, and I boarded the Milwaukee Railroad passenger train to Minneapolis. I left Albert Lea dressed for Minnesota's winter in my oxblood loafers, dark-brown wool slacks, a tan corduroy jacket, a long-sleeved blue button-down dress shirt, a Scottish plaid wool tie, and an overcoat. A few days later, after a connection in Dakar, Senegal, and then finally arriving at Freetown's Lungi International Airport, I quickly realized I was not dressed for West Africa's January weather.

In Freetown I joined six other Tanzania XIII men who had been transferred into the Sierra Leone Peace Corps Community Development/Rural Development Program, which had been designed to provide workers for building roads, bridges, wells, and schools and for giving agricultural technical assistance. Many of our activities were coordinated with the local CARE (Cooperative for American Remittances to Everywhere) program. Over time the program focus moved more and more to working with farmers in a program coordinated with Sierra Leone's agriculture department and the Food and Agriculture Organization of the United Nations to demonstrate the utility of fertilizers when growing upland or swamp rice. I eventually believed, true or not, that the gradual shifting of the program was partially due to cement, reinforcing rods, and other construction materials disappearing, whether lost, stolen, or used locally for other purposes.

Our in-country training initiation became nine weeks of immersion into the culture of Sierra Leone. The seven of us toured the country, traveling in two green Chevrolet pickups with two Peace Corps Volunteer (PCV) drivers and Nelson, a one-legged chimpanzee, the pet of one of the drivers. We were supplied with fold-up wood and canvas army cots with mosquito netting while Freetown staff scrambled to identify a posting for each of us. We learned about dry land and wetland rice cultivation, cocoa, coffee, ground nuts (peanuts), palm oil, lumber, gardening, and well, bridge, and school construction. Near the end of this period we journeyed to the north of the country, and most of us climbed Mount Bintumani, the highest peak in West Africa. We spent the final two weeks working with a seasoned volunteer to build a school in a bush village somewhere near Port Loko.

We returned to Freetown for a couple of days and awaited assignments. I went back up country when I learned I would likely be moving to the village of Binkolo.

5.

Paramount Chief Alimamy Dura II

I had a forty-year a relationship with Alimamy Dura II of the Safroko Limba Chiefdom, the Chief of Binkolo, the village I lived in most of the time I was in Sierra Leone. It began in March 1967 and continued after I left the country in December 1968 with intermittent letter writing until 1996, meeting him in Freetown in 2004, and periodic phone conversations until his death on February 23, 2007. I eventually learned he was of the Dura-Sesay family and was preceded as Chief by his father, Alimamy Dura I, and his grandfather Umaru Gbokay, a trader who immigrated from Guinea and was elected Chief of the chiefdom in 1907. I eventually learned that Alimamy Dura II was arrested by the National Provisional Ruling Council in 1993 and by the government in 1996.

Before I reconnected with Dura in 2004 I located the e-mail address of a friend who had been a Sierra Leone Peace Corps Volunteer during part of the time I had been. I sent him a short story about an African woman both of us had known. He made slight improvements to the story but thoroughly enjoyed the jolt from long ago. He wondered if I had kept in contact with any people we had known. I told him I had been in touch with Dura but lost contact with him during the Sierra Leone Civil War (1991–2002).

My fellow volunteer had served three years as a Sierra Leone PCV. Like many, he left the country exhausted. He wrote, "no contact w/SL citizens since departure, was so glad to leave, I've never looked back. Guess that third year was one too many." Three years in foreign places, at a young age, can do odd things to one. I shared his state of exhaustion when I left the country. When I told him that Dura had given me Le100 in cash (about $125) as a gift when I departed, my friend was shocked: "I actually danced up the steps of the plane at Lungi [Freetown's airport] when I left. Your Chief was sure different than either of mine. He GAVE you 50 [British West African] pounds??? Kande Souri [Chief of one of the chiefdoms my friend had lived in] was poorer than I was ... but with 32 wives, no big surprise."

I had heard of Chief Dura before I met him. But I didn't understand his importance until much later. He was one of the men who started the Sierra Leone People's Party in 1951. At his death he was the last living member of the group. He, Milton Margai (Sierra Leone's first prime minister), and one other man had been Sierra Leone Colony's representatives in London at the coronation of Queen Elizabeth II in 1953.

In the mid 1950s the colonial government determined that 12 of the 149 Paramount Chiefs were to be elected on a non-partisan basis to sit in Parliament. Dura was one of the twelve elected to Parliament. He would travel to the United States at least three times, the first in 1964. On one of these trips he flew on the Concorde. He had been in San Francisco during earthquake tremors and never forgot them. He had frequently been to Britain. He would visit South Africa and East Africa. He was sophisticated in ways I had never been exposed to.

~   ~   ~

Sierra Leone became politically independent on April 27, 1961. It retained a parliamentary system of government and membership in the British Commonwealth of Nations. Sir Milton Margai, one of the

Paramount Chief Alimamy Dura II, June 2004

founders of the Sierra Leone People's Party, became the country's first
Prime Minister after successful completion of constitutional talks in
1960. He retained that office after the country's first general election,
in May 1962, and died in 1964. Sir Albert Margai, Milton's half-
brother, succeeded him as Prime Minister and held that position until
elections in March 1967. He had attempted to establish a single-party
state but eventually dropped the idea in the face of resistance from
another group, the All People's Congress.

Between 1967 and 1969 Sierra Leone had five governments and
underwent three coups d'état. Shortly after the March 1967 election,
Siaka Stevens, who apparently won the contested election, was
appointed both Prime Minister and Mayor of Freetown by Henry
Josiah Lightfoot Boston, the Governor General, representing the

British monarchy. A few hours later Brigadier David Lansana, Commander of the Sierra Leone Military Force, put Stevens and Boston under house arrest and seized power on the grounds that the determination of the next Prime Minister should await the election of tribal representatives to Parliament. Not long after that, Brigadier Andrew Juxon-Smith threw Lansana in jail, formed the National Reformation Council, and suspended the constitution. In April 1968 a group of sergeants and corporals overthrew the National Reformation Council and formed the Anti-Corruption Revolutionary Movement, which quickly restored the democratic constitution and turned the government over to Stevens based on the 1967 election results.

After Stevens became Prime Minister he jailed Juxon-Smith, who then spent eight years in Freetown's Pademba Road Prison under a death sentence until the courts overturned his conviction. After Smith's release Stevens expelled him from the country. When security guards took him to Stevens' office to obtain his passport, the only words Stevens said to him as he handed the passport to him were "Go Bo," the words used when prisoners were to be murdered.

Juxon-Smith moved to the United States and, for a while at least, worked for the New York City Department of Finance in a low-level clerical position until Rudolph Giuliani was elected and his job was eliminated. He died in 1996 in Stapleton, New York.

In 1971, the Sierra Leone Parliament declared the country a republic. Stevens, the Prime Minister, became the country's first President of the Republic of Sierra Leone one day after the constitution was ratified. In 1978 Parliament approved a new constitution, making the country a one-party state. Stevens ruled until October 1985, when he handed over governing power to Major General Joseph Saidu Momoh, the first Sierra Leonean to achieve the rank of Major General. Momoh needed to resign his military commission to become President, which he did, ruling until April 29, 1992. Stevens died in 1988.

Momoh was overthrown in 1992 and exiled to Guinea, where he was a guest of Guinea's military government until 1996. He returned to Freetown, was found guilty of two charges of conspiracy, though not treason, and was jailed in November 1998. But he broke out of jail in January 1999 when rebel soldiers invaded Freetown. Later that year Momoh was given amnesty. He returned to Guinea, where he died on August 3, 2003. He received a state funeral in Freetown later that year. Whatever Momoh's leadership skills might have been, he also earned the nickname "Dandogo," or "fool" in the Limba language.

During my period of service, living up country, I was dimly aware of the turmoil that seemed to have become endemic in Freetown. After my January 1967 arrival, I only gradually become aware of upcoming elections, primarily by seeing and hearing political party vehicles driving through towns and blaring audio announcements encouraging people to vote. During this time there were curfews, but none seemed to affect whatever I might have been doing up country. I was dimly and naïvely aware of the tribal and regional differences that eventually helped create and fuel so much animosity, but I did not understand them at all.

~   ~   ~

I met Chief Dura when he stopped at the Peace Corps Rest House in Makeni, Sierra Leone, where I was staying before moving to Binkolo. He cheerfully approached the rest house wearing a Ben Hogan–style golf cap, Bermuda shorts, an open-necked short-sleeve shirt, and plastic loafers. He arrived driving a bright-red Alfa Romeo convertible on loan from a Lebanese trader in Freetown. (Years later I met two female ex-PCV teachers who had known the Freetown owner of the vehicle.) Dura's Mercedes was being repaired. The Chief was the only African in Binkolo who owned a vehicle. One might think owning a Mercedes excessive, but in a country where roads were mostly unpaved and not well cared for, having access to and owning a dependable vehicle was, and remains, important.

Dura, who had become Chief in 1947, was a short man, 5'6" or so, with lots of pizzazz. At forty-six years old, he was an engaging and vigorous person. He had been educated at the Bo Secondary School, a school founded in 1906 to educate sons and nominees of the Paramount Chiefs in the British manner, as they would become leaders. He had also been educated in the United Kingdom.

Because of the National Reformation Council's rule during 1967 and 1968, Alimamy Dura II likely spent more time in Binkolo than he would have otherwise, so somehow, by default, we developed a relationship we would likely not have had without the coup d'état because he would have been away on business. He seemed to like me; I enjoyed his company. He sold me his Zenith Trans-Oceanic shortwave radio and bought a Phillips shortwave radio for himself. I don't know who got the better end of the deal, but the Zenith was a godsend to me. He once gave me a fifth of Haig Scotch whiskey. He introduced me to ginger beer, to millet, and to fufu, a pounded fermented cassava root dish indigenous to Sierra Leone. He would sometimes invite me to share rice chop with him at his table or on the open-air porch of his compound, which he shared with at least three wives and their children. Often we would listen to the BBC News together and comment on whatever we heard. One time when he visited me at my rest house, he gave me a bottle of Scotch and told me I needed a haircut. Another time he offered to find me an African wife, but neither of us seriously pursued the issue.

During my Peace Corps service I met six of the Chief's wives; there may have been more. One of his Binkolo wives was Annie, the daughter of Ya Nancy Kanu, my African mother. The youngest wife I met was a very attractive woman about my age named Augusta; she was living in Freetown. She came to Binkolo at least twice while I was living there. She was planning to study medicine in Russia. She did go to Russia to become a doctor. She later worked in Czechoslovakia and eventually moved to the United States. She died of cancer in 1994.

Even though Dura was Chief and a "big man," like everyone else, he had problems. Once he had cash flow issues and asked me for a loan. I loaned him whatever it was. I have forgotten the exact amount, but it was reasonably substantial—100 leones or more. He paid me back. Our relationship was such that I did not hesitate too much to grant his request.

A pastime of many men in the village was to play draughts, a game similar to checkers but on a larger board. I enjoyed watching the men, including Dura, play. I never played, but then I was never asked to join in the game. I had been a superb checkers player in college and likely would have been a good draughts player, although the thought of squabbling with African and expatriate egos kept me from trying. If I had remained in the village longer, I would likely have jumped in and enjoyed the challenge and camaraderie.

~   ~   ~

In January 1968 I accompanied Chief Dura and Pa Kiester, a Makeni businessman, to the Koidu-Sefadu diamond mining area. Years later he labeled our journey "a reconnaissance trip."

I was also Dura's guest at the June 1968 opening ceremonies of Sierra Leone's Parliament. (The Parliament opened a few days after Robert F. Kennedy's assassination in Los Angeles, California. I was accosted on a Freetown street a day before the opening by a local man who said, "You are killing your best people.") It was a special day, and I was fortunate to be invited. We rode up the hill in Dura's white Mercedes to Government House, past exuberant crowds of market women and others superbly dressed, who were clapping, singing, shouting. I thought the country was simply ecstatic to have a new chance at democracy and self-rule.

I didn't see any other white people in the parliament building that day, although there must have been some somewhere, perhaps BBC or other media types. There was tremendous emotional electricity in the air during the ceremonies. Ibrahim Bash-Taqi, once Prime Minister Siaka Stevens' Minister of Information, was on the floor not far from Stevens himself. Bash-Taqi rose and made a comment Stevens found offensive. Stevens rose and glared at Bash-Taqi—a nonverbal response, direct and intimidating. The audience roared, "Siaka, Siaka, Siaka!" One could feel the intensity and energy of differences rising in ways I did not then imagine or think possible.

On August 30, 1974, Bash-Taqi and fourteen others were charged with treason for trying to overthrow the government. The case became known as the "Treason Trial of Mohamed Sorie Forna and fourteen others."

Forna, the first accused, had been the Minister of Finance. All were found guilty, but Stevens apparently believed executing all fifteen would cause too many problems. Stevens identified six of the men as being "of special interest." On July 19, 1975, Ibrahim Bash-Taqi and five others were hanged outside of Freetown's Pademba Road Prison. Their bodies were displayed for about an hour before they were removed. Bash-Taqi's body was buried in an unmarked grave. The surviving men were sentenced to various prison terms.

~   ~   ~

Dura and I exchanged farewells at Freetown's Paramount Hotel when I left the country in December 1968. I hadn't expected to see him. I had not been living in Binkolo, nor had I seen him, for a while. Somehow he knew when I was leaving and came to see me off. As I approached the bus to go to the airport, we shook hands in farewell, he gave me Le100 (about $125). I was surprised. I hadn't expected anything and didn't know how to refuse. By then I was so mentally and emotionally exhausted from whatever I had done or failed to do that I was eager to leave the country. I felt as if I had failed at every-thing I tried to do during my service. On my journey back to the United States I passed through Rome and Geneva. Shortly after I arrived in Geneva, I visited a jeweler, laid the money on the counter, and asked, "What kind of a watch can I get with this?" I bought a self-winding 25-jewel automatic Damas watch, which I still have as a memento of the Chief.

Not everyone liked or admired Dura; he had enemies. He was quick, and not shy about stating his opinions. Pa Mark, a friend of mine in a village not far from my house, liked Dura but also said, "He could be a scoundrel." I never asked for clarification. Mark was a delightful, short, chubby, bald farmer/preacher with a blunt stub at the end of his left arm. I thought his hand had been blown off in a hunting accident. In 2004 when I mentioned Mark's name to Dura, the Chief smiled and said, "Oh, yes, Mark!" Mark lost his hand when his shot-gun exploded during secret society ceremonies.

The female PCV school teacher who lived in Binkolo during my service respected Dura but thought him sexist at times. Many African men are, although I never saw any particularly crude behavior in my time with him. I don't know if he was crude or not regarding women, but I do know he was not shy about pursuing someone or something he wanted.

One day I accompanied him in his Mercedes into Makeni on business of some sort. I was in the back seat and he was in front with his driver. The Chief saw an attractive young woman walking down the street carrying cloth or vegetables on a platter on her head. He signaled for the driver to stop and motioned to the woman. When she came to Dura's open car window he grasped her hand and put their hands together on door's window frame. "Do ya. Do you sabe me?" (I say. Do you know who I am?)

"No," she said.

"I'm Chief Dura. I am a big man. Do you want pekin?" (Do you want to have a child by me?)

I don't know if the offer was ever consummated.

After I returned to the United States we corresponded from time to time. For some reason I never bothered to destroy some of his letters. In light of the horrible turmoil inflicted on the nation over time, his letters, few as they are, provide unique insight into some of the anguish that developed in the country again and again.

~   ~   ~

April 5, 1970

Dear Pat, Things are not bright in the country immediately. In particular I have to thank God for the life and everything we owe to him. Sierra Leone is not the one you knew from years gone by; it's quite a different place altogether as there is massive lawlessness in the place, killing each other for politic is common.

My wife asked to be remembered and all the kids. Truly yours, Chief Dura.

~   ~   ~

I wrote the Chief sometime in 1971 and mentioned a book I had recently read and suggested he might enjoy it. The book, *Back to Africa: A History of Sierra Leone and Liberia*, was written by Richard West.

> *15 January 1972*
>
> *Dear Pat, Thanks very immensely for your very kind thought towards me. As you are the very first Peace Corps who had responded in this manner to a friend in Africa. Please accept my apology for the many letters you had written to me, without a reply, one would only say that some of these letters demanded no reply because they never bear any address on them.*
>
> *I am glad to hear about your success in life I only hope God will do his grace to put more blessings upon whatever you are holding, together with your wife in life.*
>
> *The book* Back to Africa *you stated in your letter I tried to get a copy from Book Shop but there is no copy. I wonder whether you will help me to get your old used one so I can read it through.*
>
> *I had just returned from Britain where I was for three months on medical treatment. I was to go as far as the United States but I had to come home as I did not wish to remain abroad for long. Any how I wish to come over to the States sometime this year.*

I sent him the book later that year.

~   ~   ~

> *October 5, 1972*
>
> *Dear Patrick, I wish to thank you immensely for your letter, particularly for sending me that wonderful book which I have now received.*
>
> *I wish to mention here that you have really impressed me, and to say further, that you have been one of the best Peace Corps I have come across. I only do hope that you will continue your good services and friendliness you exhibited in Binkolo during your term of service as a Volunteer in Sierra Leone.*

I very much regret to have kept silence for such a long time. However, now that I have received your new address, I shall be writing to you always. Our atmosphere in the economy is now a bit improved, and things are normal. I wish success in your prediction in the election of a President in the forth-coming elections in the States. I have been out of the country for over a period of two weeks in London, and have just returned. I shall see you one day, when by chance, I visit the States.

I wish you good luck and success in the new role you have undertaken. Please extend my greetings to your friends. You will be glad to hear that a new secondary school—"Dura High School" has been opened in Binkolo during the 1972-73 school year. The school is co-educational with a roll of 150 pupils as a start.

Hoping to hear from you soon, Your friend Hon. P. C. Alimamy Dura II.

~ ~ ~

In January 1973 the Chief was detained and jailed by the Siaka Stevens government. The reasons for the jailing were not mentioned, but in 2004 the Chief told me Stevens had him jailed three times, once for "woman trouble." I did not ask him for clarification of the issue. The following letter was written after his May 1973 release.

Nov. 6, 1973

Dear Pat, Thanks ever so much for your letter of 26 May, maybe your letter without reply may have brought some luck because I was released out of detention on the 23 May where I was in a good 4 months and 10 days. However I am well both in mind and strength. Nothing is wrong with this because this is what we sometimes pay as politicians. This country is not as happy as for some years ago things are rapidly becoming Pa PA Dock. Some of my friends are still there and they have spent almost three years in detention.

May I say thanks again for the nice and interesting book Back to Africa *that all of us enjoyed while in detention and it appears pregnant with facts. I am not sure but all being well I may visit your country once more and I will surely notify you when. I was just from a tour of East Africa last year and on my return I find myself in detention. Pat be sure that in every situation there must be a savior well we are going to be, not in the too distant future.*

I wonder whether you can be of any help my son and daughter wish to go to the States to educate themselves but I have not got a place yet—if this is possible please write so that they can be there well on time for the school year. They are Sanfa R. Dura and Jane Dura they have not decided what they wish to do. Please extend my greetings to Kathy [Nardina]. Nixon ought to resign if he has any morals. But Politicians are all the same.

Pat, I shall write longer when you reply. By the way I have just opened a new secondary school in Binkolo it is The Dura high school.

Best Regards your friend P. C. Alimamy Dura.

When that letter was written I was in graduate school in Georgia and could not be of any assistance to either Sanfa or Jane. Both of them as well some of the Chief's other children eventually did get to the United States to attend school.

~   ~   ~

In 1974 I sent a children's book I had been impressed with to Dura for his children. I cannot recall what the book was about, but I also shared it with friends in the US who also had children.

6 July, 1974

Dear Pat, You are very kind for the book you sent to me for my children which they are taking full advantage of.

I hope my letters are always received as this seems a common belief that letters from this place some times never get to their destinations. I believe this because my daughter wrote to me, saying I do not reply to some of her letters which is not so.

One of your letters stated you were planning to come out again but since then I have not heard from you regarding that. Are you still interested or having some other idea? If there is anything I could do to make your coming a reality I will just be glad to help you.

I will send your address to my children so that they can get in touch with you if you don't minds.

Pat, how is life with you for we here things are really getting tough every day. Rice is 22.10 a bag you know and sugar is 5/a packet, petrol is 10/a gallon. This is killing. Please write.

Your friend, P. C. A. Dura, J.P., O.B.E.

After I attended the Friends of Sierra Leone meeting in Freetown in 2004, I learned that on June 13, 1970, Dura had been knighted, becoming an Officer of the Most Excellent Order of the British Empire (O.B.E.). When I returned to the US, I contacted the British Consulate-General in Chicago to obtain more information regarding Dura's award. My request was forwarded to the Central Chancery of the Orders of Knighthood, St. James Place, London, England, which was able to confirm the award had been given, but had no further information: "We do not have access to citations accompanying awards. In fact, in the British Honours system, these citations are not intended to either be released to the recipient, or to be made public." The Chancery referred me to the British government's Foreign and Commonwealth Office. I have yet to hear from the Office.

~ ~ ~

6 August, 1975

Thanks ever so much for your kind letter of July 2, 1975. I am glad to hear that your dear wife has given birth to a baby boy. I hope God will grant you long life and joy to enjoy him as a big boy. Nothing very badly in connection with our health. The family and myself are fine.

Things are very dare [dear] out here. Petrol is almost running to two Leone's per gallon and the rest of the commodities follow suit. So you can see, to exist is a big, big problem. However hard one got to exist.

Please extend my sincere greetings to your dear wife and son.
I wait to hear from you very soon.
    Yours very sincerely, Chief Dura II.

The economy was in a state of flux, and over time it got much worse. In 1979, at the urging of the International Monetary Fund and the World Bank, the leone was devalued. (At that time the 1 leone was more valuable than the US dollar—.80 leone equaled $1 US. In 2014 1 US dollar equaled 4,400 Sierra Leone leones. If the exchange rates had remained constant from 1979 to 2014 Le4,400 would have been valued at roughly $5,500.)

Over the next thirty-five years the economy fell into tremendous disarray. The ten years of war and the 2014–15 Ebola outbreak made things even worse. The World Health Organization reported in 2014 that Sierra Leone had the highest infant mortality rate in the world.

We continued to correspond intermittently but not often. I have lost any other letters he may have sent me during the 1980s.

~ ~ ~

During President Momoh's leadership, the nation's economy got so bad that for a time it could not afford to import gasoline or fuel oil, and the country went without electricity for months at a time. Sometime before the economy completely fell apart, Chief Dura prospered by establishing a business importing used cars from Britain and selling them in Sierra Leone.

With little understanding of what had happened in Sierra Leone during most of the 1980s, I mailed a letter to Chief Dura in June 1992. I received no response then but unexpectedly received a letter from Sierra Leone in June 1996. Having not heard from anyone from there for a long time, I was stunned, wondering who might be writing from so far away. As I looked at the envelope, I smiled and thought some guys my age could be getting a letter from West Africa with a greeting like, "Dear Dad, I am coming to America." I knew that was not possible. The letter was from Alimamy Dura II. I was very surprised with this jolt from my past.

June, 1996

Dear Pat, I am in receipt of your letter of June 1992. You may have heard there was a coup here and I was in jail until December 1995. These young boys have taken everything, even my vehicles. However I am well and God will provide.

I mailed two letters back to him, but both came back marked "Return to Sender, Service Temporarily Suspended."

6.

Binkolo

I was the first male Peace Corps Volunteer stationed in Binkolo. There are 149 chiefdoms in Sierra Leone. The village Chief, Paramount Chief Alimamy Dura II, was one of twelve chiefs elected to Sierra Leone's Parliament. Most of the chiefdom's residents were of the Limba people, the third largest group in the country.

The village is on the 60-kilometer Makeni-Kabala road. Makeni is the capital of Bombali District, and Kabala is the capital of Koinadugu District. Binkolo is a few kilometers north of Makeni, which, during my time, was a 20-cent (2-shilling) ride away. The portion of the main road through Binkolo was the only paved section of the road between the two district capitals. Dura was important enough to have arranged for an Italian-built bus connection between the village and Freetown two or three times a week.

Many village houses were of bush pole and mud construction with pan roofs made of zinc, and some were made of cement block. (A bush pole is a length of wood or a young tree branch cut to various lengths to support or frame a structure that is then filled and covered with mud.) A few had palm thatch roofs. Some were in various stages of construction. Whoever the owner was or would be was not known to me during my tour of service, and none seemed completed while I was in the village.

In its own way the village was prosperous, but from a distance many might think the place poor. It had no running water or electricity. But it was important enough for the American Wesleyan Mission to have established a primary school, for boys only, during the 1920s. During my time of service the primary school had approximately 140 students, still mostly boys.

Commerce was primarily agricultural. Tsetse flies prohibited the raising of cattle in the chiefdom, but Fullah cattle raisers a few kilometers north supplied cattle to be butchered in the village three days a week. Items available at the small shop operated by a chubby Muslim farmer/proprietor included kerosene for lantern and stove, rice, flour, sugar, salt, palm oil, and Vimto—an extraordinarily sweet cola-like drink.

On the ground in front of his shop, women, sitting on open-air benches and stools, sold groundnuts, oranges, kola nuts, mangoes, cassava root, cassava leaf, potato leaf greens, pineapple, and bonga (dried fish) for rice chop. A baker sold a French-type loaf, which he baked in an earthen oven, but it dried out quickly. Once he asked me to purchase some bread pans for him during one of my visits to Freetown. I foolishly never got around to helping him on his venture. Periodically a woman sold frozen red snapper from a 40-kilo box shipped by lorry from Freetown. One had to be prompt to purchase the fish, as it thawed and was eventually covered with flies and dust from the nearby road.

Makeni, was near enough for one to enjoy some of the benefits of a larger city: electricity; cinema; Barclay's Bank; a dispensary and hospital; churches and mosques; government offices; running water; a large, roofed open market for meats, fruits, and vegetables; library; post office; Choithrams grocery store, stocked with some imported goods and staffed by Indians. Other commerce included shops operated by African or Lebanese shopkeepers, a wood and ivory carver named Momodu Kanneh, an active garra cloth industry, a restaurant with take-out that sold Lebanese-type food, passenger railroad transport to Freetown, and other transportation services to various parts of the country. (Garra cloth was an imported white cloth tied into regular patterns and soaked in indigo, brown, red, or green dye.)

In Binkolo one could enjoy the isolation and solitude of village life and savor the rhythms of the agricultural economy. The village's location enabled one to move back and forth to Makeni without too much difficulty as long as one did not wait too late in the day, when public transport services became unlikely or impossible

I was not nearly as isolated as some PCVs. My contact with the non-village world was primarily through a Zenith Transoceanic shortwave radio, hearsay from anyone I encountered, mail delivered three times a week (when I received copies of *Time*, *Newsweek*, the *National Catholic Reporter*, and family mail), and intermittent trips to Freetown, where from time to time I purchased the latest edition of the *Economist*.

7.

The Rest House, My Home

My village home was a cream-colored, zinc pan-roofed, rectangular, cement block building on the crest of a hill overlooking parts of the village. The house was about 75 yards from the road to the village. A narrow red dirt path, for walkers and the rarely motorized vehicle, was the main way from my home to the village. In 2004 Dura mentioned the name of my landlord, Pa Pasang. I believe that in my naïveté I never met the owner while I was there, but he may have been the fellow I helped use bush poles and metal sheets to frame my bathing and latrine area. In hindsight I was a source of money for the village in ways I did not then understand. I lived in the village rest house.

The rest house was well built. It was near the village, but I thought of sufficient distance from other housing to signify use by someone not from the village. It was vacant and unfurnished when I moved in. The building's zinc roof maximized the heat from the sun during the dry season and reinforced the power and rage of the tropical rains during the six-month rainy season. Parts of the roof shook and rattled violently in the forceful harmattan and monsoon winds of the transition period between the dry and rainy seasons, as well as during the rainy season storms. A corner porch overlooked the village. At times, particularly during the dry season, the sunsets in the dusty air were spectacular. The sun would drop quickly into the horizon through the serene haze from wood cooking smoke and harmattan dust, and the branches of palm, mango, orange, and lemon trees while the motor sound of lorries passing through the village echoed up the hill. I often heard the sound of women beating rice in wooden mortars with pestles, preparing for a later meal. It was a pleasant and peaceful place once I settled into the routine of a new home. I was young and dumb, and over time I began to love the place.

The rest house, my home, was the only village building with glass windows—six, French louvered. The house had three exterior doors, all painted dark blue. Two Dutch doors opened to the porch. The third door, the back door, led to my latrine and bathing area, as well as an adjacent bush path to farms and nearby villages.

A few steps from the back door was a small rectangular shed, likely built as a kitchen. I used it for storage. I was my own cook, and I cooked inside the house. The Peace Corps book locker's *Fanny Farmer Cookbook* was a godsend. (Book lockers were large cardboard boxes supplied to all volunteers. They were full of a variety of fiction and nonfiction and were provided to help us fill some of our time while we adjusted to living in new cultures. I did not get a new book locker but received one left when a PCV who had finished their tour of service left Sierra Leone.) Outside the back door, near the corner of the house, was my water supply, a 50-gallon drum that gathered water from the roof's gutter spout during the rainy season. The drum stored water for cooking, bathing, and drinking. I boiled water and poured it into in a two-level 2½-gallon cylinder with two balloon chalk-like water filters for my cooking and drinking water. During the dry season, school-boys hauled water to me to earn school fees. (School fees varied from school to school and paid for such things as uniforms, books, and incidentals needed at a school.) As the dry season lengthened and the water table got lower, the water retained more laterite sediment and the filters were often covered with red gunk after the water filtered through them.

The rest house, my Binkolo home, in 1967

The rest house was two rooms partitioned into four by bush poles with plywood-like sheets attached to them to create a bedroom, a living room, a small storage space, and a larger room for cooking and eating.

I hung a mirror and calendar between the kitchen's rear door and east window. Beneath the mirror was a small table where I shaved in the morning. The table also served as the food preparation and clean up area.

One might think the house sparse. It may have been, but it became my home. I furnished the kitchen with a three-burner kerosene stove, a portable oven to fit over the stove, a kerosene fridge, a wooden armoire for a pantry, a small table by the back door to hold the water filter, a kerosene lantern, and a large metal bowl that served as my kitchen sink for washing dishes and as my bathtub for nightly bathing in the latrine area. My final pieces of kitchen furniture were an oblong table and four chairs. The table could accommodate four persons for dinner, although no more than two others ever ate with me at the table. The table also served as an ironing board when Foday Kamara, my housekeeper, ironed laundry with a charcoal-heated iron.

All my washed clothing needed to be ironed in order to kill any putzi fly (or, tumbu fly) eggs that might have been laid in the cloth when it was hung out to dry. Otherwise, the eggs would hatch upon contact with human skin and the larvae would burrow into the skin and develop into maggots, which can result in boil-like sores. Usually I kept the table covered with a piece of country cloth I had purchased during my travels. Over time I fancied up the place with curtains over the windows.

I cleaned the pantry armoire regularly. I determined the proper cleaning time by the size and number of cockroaches that scurried for cover whenever the pantry door was opened. The kerosene fridge's flue was sensitive and had to be kept level in order for the internal elements to work and enable the heated chemicals to cool and freeze water in small ice trays. If not properly tuned or kept clear of soot, air movement could blow out the flame and the fridge wouldn't work. It was not uncommon to find drowned ants in the small ice tray inside the fridge.

Many mornings, while listening to the BBC African Service, I prepared pancakes made in part from KLIM, a powdered milk product. I also used Danish butter from a tin, as well as Tate and Lyle's Golden Syrup. Over time, black ants would linger near the top of the syrup can. During my second year I purchased, in Freetown, twelve or twenty-four paper cartons of milk from Denmark. The milk was packaged in some way to prevent spoilage and was a wonderful luxury for a Minnesota farm boy.

About 20 yards from my back door was a 9' by 9' cement floor partitioned into two areas: one for latrine, one for bathing. There were no walls or roof when I moved in. A rectangular wooden box served as the toilet stool. Periodically I dumped fresh lime powder into the pit. Early on, relieving my bowels was truly an open exhibition.

When the previous resident moved away, material for the walls and roof had been removed for other purposes. A day or so after I moved in, the Chief had a man cut bush poles for framing the structure. We nailed up zinc panels for the sides and roof. I never bothered to attach a door to either doorway. I had thoughts of having a 25-gallon drum put on stilts over the bathing area for a shower, but with no available running water and the need to haul water from my rain barrel, a local stream, or a distant well, and then pour it into a raised drum, I never completed that task. My bath during the dry season was pleasant, sun-warmed water drawn from the 50-gallon drum. During

The latrine and bathing area
at the rest house when I moved into Binkolo

the rainy season the water from the roof spout was cleaner than water hauled during the dry season, but it could get quite chilly. The PCV teacher who moved to Binkolo after me was a woman. I do not know what changes she may have made to the bathing and latrine area if she continued to live at the rest house.

My bedroom had a single bed shrouded with hanging mosquito netting. I had an armoire for clothing, a rectangular metal travel locker, and a bedside cardboard box, where I placed my shortwave radio. I often woke during the night and turned the radio on for news from around the world. I heard of student riots in Paris in 1967; the 1967 fires and race riots in Detroit; the Russian invasion of Czechoslovakia in August 1968; and the Six-Day War between Israel and Egypt. I heard of riots at the 1968 democratic convention in Chicago and of Black Panthers exiting the student union at Cornell University in Ithaca, New York, armed with weapons. I heard of the murder of Martin Luther King Jr. in Memphis in April 1968. And later that night I listened to the Voice of America broadcast of Robert F. Kennedy's Indianapolis, Indiana, speech, delivered from the back of a flatbed truck, hoping there would not be riots after the shooting. I later heard of the murder of Robert Kennedy in June 1968.

Mosquito netting, to protect against mosquitoes carrying malaria, hung over and around my bed. The netting had been ripped during our nine-week in-service and cross-country orientation, and I never bothered to replace it with new netting. It didn't seem to be a major concern, even though I had at least two horrible, incapacitating days of chills, nightmares, and ennui during a malarial attack.

My living room was supplied with four wooden lounge chairs, a low oblong table, and a cardboard Peace Corps book locker retrieved from somewhere when an earlier PCV left the country. Over time I had three or four flat oval baskets used for winnowing rice hung on a wall for decoration. As part of our in-country orientation the Peace Corps gave many of us a white-covered geography book about Sierra Leone. I kept it displayed on the table; sometime during my stay it was stolen.

~   ~   ~

The Camel Back rock formation north of Binkolo

Early in my second dry season I planted impatiens flowers under the eaves on two sides of the house. They were bountiful and beautiful. I found them attractive—a touch of domesticity, I thought.

Schoolboys told me I was foolish for planting the flowers. When I asked why, they said, "Snakes can hide there." Areas around most village buildings were bare dirt. Boys and men used machetes to keep any foliage near a building short or non-existent. After my encounters with a couple of green mambas, a python, and a snake bite that required hospitalization, I had a greater appreciation for the schoolboys' point of view. When I returned to the village in 2004, Momoh Dura, one of Alimamy Dura II's sons, reminded me that the flowers and the possibility of snakes had frightened schoolboys enough that they stayed away from my home more often than not.

Through one kitchen window I could see a sloping field of okra and potato leaf, and cassava, banana, and papaya plants. Down the slope were 600 acres that had been cleared and planted with oil palm seedlings. The seedlings were in their second or third year of growth—small. If one didn't know better one might have thought it was simply a large field of elephant grass.

When I looked through the other kitchen window, I could see, a few miles away, "Takabla" (Massive Thing), the Camel Back—an aptly named steeply humped rock formation that signals the beginning of the hilly and mountainous terrain that eventually leads to Mount Bintumani.

From the corner porch, down the hill, through cassava plants, and mango and palm trees, I could see the village and the home of Pa Tamba Kargbo and his wives, Yenki and Yabu, and their children. Their house was a large rectangular mud building with a corrugated zinc roof. It abutted a dirt road leading to small farming villages. I often saw and heard Yenki and Yabu pounding rice in their wooden mortars or preparing various rice chop meals in their zinc pan–roofed, open-air, bush pole–walled kitchen, with wood fire and stone stove, not far from their back door.

Near my porch was a scrawny mango tree and an almost as scrawny palm tree. I once photographed my housekeeper, Foday, as he climbed the palm tree to demonstrate the technique of tapping its bulbous top to seep palm wine into a calabash.

If I looked past and over Tamba's roof I could see a knoll in the village where cattle, raised by Fullah herdsmen to the north, were butchered and sold three times a week. The village was a good posting; beef was not as readily accessible in many other parts of the country. Often, but always on butchering mornings, vultures perched patiently on nearby rooftops. During the beef sale one could hear the raspy sounds of their talons and wings as they glided to rest on zinc rooftops to survey the territory and espy a meal of bovine remnants left by the butcher. Vultures are wonderful scavengers and effective at keeping unsightly debris out of sight. They are ugly, but there can be a charm in any animal, even vultures at times. Some of my negative preconceived notions of vultures were gradually eliminated as they became part of the local color.

~ ~ ~

What happened in the house? To save my sanity in this semi-isolation minority status—or to regain it—I cooked. I became good at it. I wrote. I played solitaire. I listened to shortwave radio: the BBC World and African Service, the Voice of America, the Armed Forces Radio and Television Service, the Canadian Broadcasting Corporation, Radio South Africa, Deutsche Welle, Radio Moscow, and other stations around the word. I ate breakfast listing to the BBC's African Service and the strains of "Lillibullero," an Irish marching tune, the BBC's musical lead into the news at the top of each hour. The Armed Forces Radio and Television Service broadcast major league baseball games and a delightful sports talk program from WBZ, a Boston radio station. It also broadcast short segments from radio stations around the US. Once I heard a segment from Minneapolis/St. Paul's WCCO. I was so appreciative of the segment that I wrote a letter to the station. A distant relative of mine worked there and forwarded the letter to my family.

I especially enjoyed the Voice of America's Willis Conover, who broadcast *Music USA* and the *Voice of America Jazz Hour* six nights a week. *Music USA*, at 6:30 PM in my time zone, was half an hour of the music of Jim Webb and popular American songwriters and singers of that ilk. The *Voice of America Jazz Hour*, at 8:15, was 45 minutes of jazz led in with the sound of Duke Ellington's "Take the A Train." It was repeated two hours later for other time zones. Conover's programs were a godsend, and a primer of American music: Armstrong, Fitzgerald, Ellington, Monk, Davis, Brubeck, Mingus, and Tatum, and others.

I also thoroughly enjoyed the VOA's French service broadcast of African music with the announcer Georges Collinet—he was energetic. Without too much effort one could develop a good musical ear. Nightly I heard music I had not been able to hear much of when I lived in Minnesota, and I loved it! I eventually met Collinet at the National Peace Corps Association 40+1 meeting in 2002 in Washington, DC. He was born in Cameroon, came to the US in 1959 to produce a film, and ended up staying. He worked with African musicians in Paris during the '70s and '80s, hosted *Afropop* and *Afropop Worldwide*, and co-created the Maracas d'Or, the African music equivalent of the Grammys.

8.

Eviction

When I arrived in Freetown in 1967 I and a few of my Tanzania XIII friends were lodged at the (downtown) Peace Corps Rest House. On our first or second day in the country we were walking on a busy street near our lodging. Anyone who saw us could easily tell, by our dress and demeanor, that we were strangers to the country. Many young kids approached us saying, "Porto, porto. Give me penny. Give me penny!" ("Porto" is a Krio term meaning "foreigner" or "white man." It is derived from "Portuguese.") One of us was wearing a watch with a flexible wrist band. A young boy grabbed the wristband, ripped it from my friend's arm, and ran off. I ran after him, grabbed him by the neck, and retrieved the watch. Onlookers crowded around and chastised the youth for the attempted theft. Not having a wristwatch of my own, I was not as disturbed by the theft attempt as was my friend. Regardless, one way or another, each of us likely became immediately aware that any initial assumption of an across-the-board welcome as a guest in Sierra Leone would need to be adjusted. Over time, whatever thoughts we left the United States with and brought to Sierra Leone were adjusted again and again.

I was robbed the first or second day I moved into Binkolo. A schoolboy entered my new home and stole the pants to my dress suit. I had not attached a padlock to the main door, thinking I didn't need one. I quickly reported the theft to Chief Dura and Sergeant Saidu, the police officer. The pants were quickly retrieved, and the foolish boy punished. I never saw the youth again. I was shocked by the theft and was uneasy. I had expected a smoother welcome.

A second theft occurred a year or more later. I noticed that the book of the geography of Sierra Leone the Peace Corps office had given to all PCVs had disappeared from my home. At that time the book theft was a minor annoyance, but in a small way it reinforced the message that I was a visitor, a guest of the country.

One night, not long after the pants theft, I was lying in my bed and heard an odd crunch sound coming up the laterite path from the village. I lifted the mosquito netting from my bed and peered out the window. A strange light, not a flashlight or a kerosene or gas lantern, was approaching. Crunch, crunch, crunch. I became increasingly uneasy. What or who was it? Was it one or many? What was going on? Was I safe? My paranoia from moving to West Africa at a time of racial strife in the US increased. I was a stranger in a new place, and alone in a way I had never been before.

Soon the crunch maker passed the window. "Kushe, Kushe," he said—"hello" in Krio. "Kushe," I said in response. He was a hunter, and he had a burning candle and tin reflector attached to his forehead. He was seeking duiker, a small deer sometimes seen in the bush. He was looking for food. The crunch was the sound his rubber tire tread sandals made as he walked on the loose soil. This was part of my initiation into my new home.

I had a more pleasant initiation a few weeks later. It was a rite of passage for most expatriates to have a local tailor sew African clothing for them. For men that usually meant a tie-dyed garra cloth one-piece collarless shirt; for women, a two- or three-piece garra cloth dress with a blouse, wrap-around skirt, and matching head scarf. I believe I had tailors make more shirts for me than any volunteer I knew. One shirt I often wore for festive events was a blue, green, and kola nut (brown)–dyed shirt cut in a style a tailor in Makeni suggested— "Beatles style," mimicking the collarless jackets worn on the *Love Me Do* album cover. The hem's length could vary depending on the style determined by the tailor or specified by the buyer.

Not long after I moved into Binkolo I bought a speckled blue and brown lappa (a 4' by 6' piece of dyed garra cloth) from Saffie Daramy, a garra cloth merchant in Makeni. I asked a tailor a couple of doors from her shop to sew me a shirt. When he asked what length of hem I wanted I impulsively suggested a hem longer than the ones he had earlier made for me. It was a fortuitous and wonderful choice. The first time I wore the shirt in the village I was astonished by the reception. As I walked the road, villagers came to their front stoops, bowed, clasped their hands or applauded, shouting "Alahoy, alahoy!" (Wonderful, wonderful! in Limba). I quickly learned the shirt was in the style and length worn by Limba tribesmen. I had passed a significant milestone and felt accepted in the village.

More than a year later, I left the village suddenly and under duress.

I had been working with a UN Food and Agriculture Organization project that promoted hybrid rice seed and fertilizer donated by West Germany and selected fertilizer demonstration sites during the upland rice growing season, the rainy season. My work involved walking to villages, finding the village head man, and arranging to return to speak to him and to area farmers at a later date about the availability of rice and fertilizer and how much they might afford to buy for the upcoming growing season. It was time-consuming work. I put a lot of effort into it. I obtained many orders for seed. When I took the chiefdom's order to the district's agricultural officer, he laughed at me. I had apparently requested half of the seed available to the entire province.

Once, during my second trip to one of the villages to meet with farmers, a woman from village I had never visited was in my audience. She was impressed with what she understood of my message and wanted me to go to her village. When I finished speaking to the farmers it was getting late in the afternoon; I could either say thank you to them and to the woman, walk back to Binkolo, and later try to find her village, or go with her and hope I could make it home before dark.

She enthusiastically encouraged me to accompany her. I did. She was a fast walker, even compared to me. We took off on a bush path and went over and down a hill to a pleasant valley with a stream and near level fields, which held promise for a good rice yield in the upcoming rainy season. During our walk we met an older woman working in a field, smoking a pipe. I was amused, never having seen a woman smoking a pipe before. My female guide's village, accessible only by bush paths, consisted of approximately twenty mud-block homes with grass roofs surrounded by a fence of bush poles and an elephant-grass border. A small corral of some type, for domestic animals, was near one side of the village. There had been a fire, and many of the homes' grass roofs had been destroyed and were being repaired before the upcoming rainy season.

The woman located the village head man, who gathered other village men to meet me. I introduced myself as Mr. Pat or Mr. Patrick from Binkolo. I emphasized I was a Peace Corps Volunteer and was working to bring seed rice into the chiefdom. More than once I repeated "Peace Corps this" and "Peace Corps that," trying to grasp whether any of the men knew what the Peace Corps was. My Krio wasn't bad, but my Limba and Temne were poor for trying to explain my mission. After a while the village head man beckoned for me to follow him. He led me to the village latrine, presumably believing I needed to relieve my bladder.

I later started walking back to Binkolo, but it was getting near dark and I knew it would be a long walk if I returned on the bush paths I had used to reach this village. The road between Kabala and Binkolo went in a different direction from those paths. I took off on a bush path I had never been on in search of the road. I reached the road. It was almost dark. I flagged down a vehicle to get a lift to Binkolo. It was dark when I got back to Binkolo. The wife of the Muslim shop keeper down the hill from my home was sitting on her porch with a kerosene lantern next to her when I got out of the lorry. She was surprised to see me arriving in Binkolo at that time of day. And she was stunned when I told her where I had been. Looking at me, she said something like, "Kushe for waka"—"Thank you for doing that, for walking that far." I got home in time to listen to Willis and the *Voice of America Jazz Hour.*

~   ~   ~

Seed rice was later delivered to my home in 50-kilogram (110-pound) bags. Word quickly spread that rice was available. I was inundated with farmers—some I knew, others I had never met. In my naïveté I rushed to get the rice to farmers for the upcoming rice season. A farmer and a young man would appear at my door seeking the rice seed. Quickly the bag, the helper—carrying the bag on his head—and the farmer would disappear down a bush path to return to village and farm. I thought I was doing well. When the upland rice growing season began I had established eighteen UN Food and Agriculture Organization fertilizer sites. I had distributed hybrid rice seed. I had gotten to parts of the chiefdom and to farmers I had not worked with during the previous year. I was looking forward to a successful conclusion of my tour of service.

Midway through my second dry season I knew I wanted photos of chiefdom people I had become close to before I left the country. Knowing I would be leaving soon I spent a few days going from village to village, farm to farm, locating friends and taking pictures of them with the Kodak Instamatic my family had given me when I graduated from college. On the way back to my home I took a photo of Ya Nancy, my African mother, and later passed the home of A. J. Sesay, the new Headmaster of the local primary school. I had met him a few times, but we did not know each other well. He had recently moved into the village, and we were yet to work with each other. As I neared his home there was a slight drizzle in the late-afternoon light. Two of his kids were standing in the rain water spewing from a roof gutter on his house. The sunlight was especially good. I took a photo of his kids, who were wearing no clothes.

Soon A. J. approached my home, protesting I had taken a photo of his naked kids. He charged I would return to America to show the photo and make fun of how primitive the people were, and so on.

I protested that his allegation was not my intent. I said I had been taking photos of people I was fond of, photos of people I wanted to have when I returned to America. I apologized for any harm he might have felt. I assured him that no disrespect was intended. I said the photo of his children couldn't be destroyed, as the negative was in a cartridge. He was not satisfied. He left my home in a huff. I hoped that was the end of the story. It was not.

A few days a later, in the harmattan heat, I was home reading. A black mini-Morris motored up the path to my home. (The mini-Morris was a small economy car built by the British Motor Corporation). The driver was E. M. Kargbo, the District Education Officer, and along with him was A. M. Sesay, the previous Headmaster of Binkolo's primary school. A. M. was E. M.'s new deputy. Accompanying Kargbo were Pa Fanka (Binkolo's head man) and A. J. Sesay. Chief Dura was not in the village at the time.

A. J. was still angry and wanted resolution of the photograph issue in his favor. He repeated his charges. I asked the others to support me but to no avail. In anger I rashly grasped the camera, opened it, removed the film cartridge, twisted the cartridge, and threw it onto my garbage heap.

I was moved from the village. I was removed from an un-winnable position. My UN work with chiefdom farmers would be un-recordable. A. J. had been in the village a short time. He may have been trying to establish his turf. He was following A. M., a well-respected school headmaster. A. J. may have been trying to indicate to the village that he was not one to be trifled with. He may have thought I would actually do what he had charged. He may have thought I liked to take photos of naked kids. He may have been suspicious of me because I had not developed a sexual relationship with any woman in the village.

What might the others have thought? I knew each of them. They may not have believed A. J.'s charges. Even if they did believe me, what were their choices? They likely needed to support A. J. regardless of what they thought of the charges. Even if A. J. was a fool, someone had to save face. Someone of importance had appointed him to his new position, and he would be in the village longer than me—I was scheduled to leave in a few months. I was easier to discard regardless of whatever issues were between any of them and me.

I had been foolish and impetuous. I could have saved the negatives in the cartridge from the garbage and developed prints when I returned to America.

Whatever happened during that incident with A. J., my actions were not too serious to some. Years later Chief Dura phoned me from Freetown one morning and raised the A. J. issue. He stated how upset he had been when he returned to the village and learned I had been removed and mentioned how annoyed he had been with A. J.'s arrogance. The Chief chuckled and said, "A. J. is the example of a half-educated African man."

~ ~ ~

In 2006, my wife had knee-replacement surgery and was convalescing at a health care center in West St. Paul, Minnesota. One day while I was visiting her I greeted a young orderly and asked his name and where he was from. The young man said his name was Kargbo and that he was from Freetown, Sierra Leone. I told him I knew Freetown and had recently been there. I mentioned I knew Makeni. He stated he knew Makeni. I asked if he knew someone named E. M. Kargbo. The orderly's eyes lit up, and he replied that E. M. was one of his uncles and had been the Provincial Education Officer. We talked a bit more. The orderly told me that in 1997 his family had fled Freetown by boat to Guinea. They were on the ocean for three or four days and ran out of water before reaching Conakry, Guinea; several passengers died while on that boat.

~ ~ ~

The event that precipitated my removal from the village was painful, but I had been at fault in another matter a few months before that.

Foday Kamara, my housekeeper, was a very good fellow—a hard worker even though his work for me was not taxing. He did my laundry and dishes, and guarded my home when I was away. The local female Peace Corps teacher hired Foday to do some work on her home not long before she was scheduled to leave the village. Sometime during her stay in the village she lost her college graduation ring. She was upset about the loss. She was even more upset when she noticed Foday wearing the ring. She accused him of being a thief. Foday denied the accusation, saying he had found the ring. His response did not soothe her anger.

I was at a loss for what to do in the matter. If indeed Foday had found the ring, I thought he should have been wise enough to realize it belonged to an expatriate and sharp enough to at least not wear it until the teacher had moved from the village. I felt I had to support the Peace Corps teacher, rather than simply talk to Foday, ask him to return the ring, and give him a "dash" (that is, money) as gratitude from having found the ring. But I fired Foday and employed schoolboys to do the work he had done for me.

Both I and the female teacher were impetuous in this event. Neither of us had the wisdom or patience to speak with village elders or other people we respected and ask for advice. By the time of the incident she had been in the country twenty or more months and I had been there a few months less. That length of time away from family and friends, being young, living as a minority, being lonely, struggling, and trying to learn what adulthood might mean or become for either of us affected our decision making. But whatever caused me to make the decisions I did, I wish I had been able to make different ones. Foday was a good fellow, and it was no fault of his that he did not have as many life choices as I did or would likely have in the future.

9.

Driving Record

Peace Corps Volunteers can no longer obtain a driver's license from their host country during their service. This was not the policy when I was a PCV. My Sierra Leone driving record is probably one of the reasons such a policy was adopted.

I did not kill or maim anyone while driving in Sierra Leone. I was never jailed. I did not have the experience of a community development PCV who rolled his green Chevrolet pickup on a bush road somewhere in the north of the country. (After the rollover, local lorry drivers and others stopped in the blocked road to stare, to palaver, and to help the PCV driver. Other than a dent in the cab's roof, the pickup was unharmed. The PCV driver and others up righted the vehicle. The PCV thanked those who helped him and continued on his journey. When we were at the Makeni Peace Corps Rest House later, he wryly said, in his Carolina drawl, "It was might white of those fellows to help me out.")

Nor did I have an experience like the PCV who fainted while driving a Chevrolet pickup in downtown Freetown and ran into a local doctor's vehicle. Fortunately, no one was hurt in that encounter either.

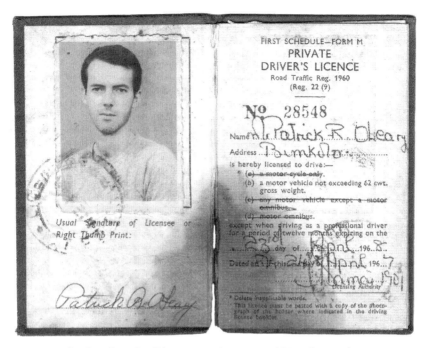

In this photo I will be twenty-three years old in a few weeks.
I am wearing a short-sleeve gray athletic shirt. I have a day's growth
of beard, a full head of dark hair, combed and parted on the right.
I am slightly over 6'1". I weigh 152 pounds. In twenty months,
when I leave the country, I will weigh 141 pounds.

I drove a Peace Corps vehicle prior to obtaining a Sierra Leone
driver's license. I did so because I wanted a bed. When I moved into
Binkolo I had been in the country for almost four months and had
been sleeping on my second foldout army cot more often than not.
I like to sleep on a good bed. My first cot became ruined when the
canvas ripped and my butt began to hang low into the wooden frame,
lower than I wanted it to. When I moved into a new home in Binkolo,
I was tired of sleeping on a cot and wanted a real bed.

Peace Corps staff in two vehicles escorted me into the village in
mid April. One vehicle was left, with its keys, at my new home while
my escorts continued north on some other task. I quickly drove to

Makeni to retrieve a bed frame, box spring, and mattress. A day or two later I drove to Makeni to purchase more groceries. On the way back to Binkolo, the vehicle ran out of gas. I was almost immediately met by the returning Peace Corps staff. They put fuel into the stalled vehicle, took me back my new home, and then drove the vehicle to Makeni. The incident was embarrassing but seemed of little consequence. I received a Sierra Leone driver's license a few days later.

More than a year later I ran over a pregnant cow. It was a true bit of foolishness and probably a bit of arrogance. I had escorted new PCV teachers, a husband and wife, and their supplies to their posting. Returning, in the dark, to Makeni, I encountered a herd of cattle being driven across or down the road. One cow spooked and ran in front of the vehicle. I could not stop—the vehicle may not have had working brakes—and I drove over the cow. I was driving a green fourwheel-drive Chevrolet pickup with raised axles. The Peace Corps had the only such vehicles in the country, so they were readily identifiable. I didn't have much money with me. I didn't bother to stop, confident that the cattle owner would contact Peace Corps personnel in Makeni for resolution of any issues related to the death of the cow.

A few days later I was at the Peace Corps manager's Makeni house when a man wearing a long dusty djellaba (a long, loose, hooded full cloak worn by many Muslims) and an embroidered small hat approached the house. He was the Fullah cattleman, wanting payment for his dead cow. One could tell he was resolute and important by the way he handled himself. He informed us that someone had run over his pregnant cow and had not stopped to talk to him about the incident. Agreement on damages was reached: Le50 for the cow, Le5 for the unborn calf—about $90.

My later mishap with a Volkswagen Beetle was more serious. I was involved in a four-day trek with my Peace Corps supervisor and the provincial Chief Education Officer. We drove two vehicles to meet education officials to arrange living and working sites for incoming PCV school teachers. We spent the first night in Kamakwie, the second in Kambia. Our third day became a long one. We had to a leave in time to reach a ferry on the Little Scarcies River before dark in order to return to Kamakwie. We had spent the second night eating, drinking, and palavering with the local officials in Kambia. I was not an important functionary in the negotiations. The next day I wanted to head back to the ferry before our Peace Corps leader did; I was anxious to get to the ferry.

We finally left for the ferry. I was driving the lead vehicle. We were on a good but narrow dirt road bordered by hand-dug drainage ditches edged by tall yellow savannah grass and intermittent scrub hardwood trees.

Midway in the journey I approached a gradual curve and dip in the road. Suddenly I met an oncoming white Volkswagen Beetle with a male driver and two female passengers. Both of us swerved to avoid the other, but my left front fender nicked the left rear fender of the Beetle, which stopped in the ditch, tipped partially on its side.

I stopped, got out, and ran back to the Volkswagen. No one was harmed, but the Volkswagen driver was incensed. Seeing that they were safe, I ran back up the road to flag down the other Peace Corps driver to prevent a more serious mishap. By now the Volkswagen driver was even angrier with me. He accused me of being a bad and reckless driver. In truth, both of us had likely been driving too fast on what we expected to be an empty road.

It was agreed that I would continue to the ferry and to Kamakwie to contact the authorities and return with them in the morning. The other parties in this event would remain at the accident scene to await authorities in the morning. Some time later I appeared at the provincial court in Makeni. There was a fine and a settlement of some sort. Whether I was a recipient of good will, good insurance, good fortune, or good grace, I didn't know then and I don't know now. I do remember feeling comforted that no one was seriously harmed and that I wasn't particularly concerned about the court appearance.

10.

Driver Ants

FAMILY *Formicidae*
SUBFAMILY *Dorylinae*
TRIBE *Dorylini*
GENUS *Dorylus*

In the tropical rainforest, ants are common. They are the most abundant of animals. Their total biomass, or how much they would weigh if gathered together, is greater than any other group of animals in the rainforest.

Colonies of driver ants, a type of sightless ant found in parts of Africa, can survive a flash flood and travel for days by water. It is common to encounter inch-wide trails of driver ants crossing roads or bush paths. Ant colonies can reach sizes of up to 50 million individuals. Driver ants are swarm raiders, with up to two million workers in a leading swarm. They can move 20 meters per hour. They eat insects, arthropods, earthworms, plants, and small vertebrates, and they have been known to kill tarantulas, lizards, birds, snakes, pigs, and some larger animals. Driver ants are nomads and move every three weeks to two months. They are of little danger to humans and other mammals, although they can bite pretty hard. The queen driver ant holds the record for being the largest ant in the world.

As I walked bush paths I often came across lines of driver ants devouring remnants of whatever part of the food chain had come into their path. As long as I kept moving I was in no danger from the ants, but I often had thoughts of the story "Leiningen versus the Ants," a short story I had read in junior or senior high school written by Carl Stephenson about a plantation owner in Brazil whose land was invaded by an enormous horde of ants. Often in the back of my mind I had visions from Jonathan Swift's *Gulliver's Travels*, too—of being stuck somewhere with ants crawling over my body and not being able to get away and being eaten to death. I was dimly aware of their potential viciousness and wanted to avoid them.

Whenever I came across driver ants on a bush path I simply stepped over their line and went on my merry way.

Driver ants invaded my home twice. I often awoke thirsty during the night. I would leave my bed and go to my kitchen/dining room for a drink of cold water from my kerosene fridge. One night as I was doing this I felt a strange biting sensation on my bare feet. Puzzled, I lit my kerosene lantern. The floor was inundated with driver ants. The ants had come across the porch, under the front door, and into my home. Driver ants usually follow their leader like a convoy, passing over terrain until they come across edible plant or animal matter. Although Foday and I kept my place clean, I suspect now, years later, that the head ant might have been attracted by fragments of food detritus not thoroughly swept away.

By this time I had lived in the village for many months and I was either too tired or too jaundiced to be very upset by this intrusion. I retrieved my 5-gallon drum of fuel and poured some of the kerosene on the invaders, who wildly searched for an exit or other salvation. I wiped my feet to remove the ones that had bitten me, now dead, and retreated to bed. In the morning I swept away ant remnants. There were a lot of them.

I had a second encounter with driver ants while in the village that was more public and embarrassing. I have a long association with chickens. I can remember raising chickens when I was three or four years old. When we moved to the farm, when I was seven, my family quickly started raising more.

In the spring we would purchase baby chicks from a hatchery and keep them in the heated basement of our house in a small pen with a heating lamp, food, and water. We would later move them to an outside chicken coop with chicken mesh wire, egg-carton dividers, shredded newspaper, loose straw, and an infrared heating lamp to keep the chicks warm. As their weight increased, the size of the pen was gradually increased until the chicks no longer needed such artificial support.

Dad and I were the butchers. Sometimes Dad simply wrung their necks by grasping the chicken's neck and whirling the chicken's body until the head and trunk separated. I always used an ax. Dad and his crew of assorted helpers—his eleven children—would scald the chickens in hot water, pluck their feathers, gut them, cut them up, rinse them, and put them into plastic bags for the freezer or save them for supper.

After I had lived more than a year in the village I began to raise chickens. Chickens had an important and symbolic place in African life. The gift of a chicken was a sign of a special friendship, and a healthy chicken was a prized possession. Village chickens were more often than not free-range, scrawny, and tough. They became that way due to the many enemies they faced, including snakes and driver ants.

I had observed a Makeni chicken-growing business. The owner's chicken coop was a large screened building with a water trough around the exterior foundation of the building. The trough was a barrier to drown ants that might try to enter the coop. In Binkolo I built a raised chicken coop three or four feet above the ground with bush poles and bamboo. I placed the pole corners into the ground but did not have any type of a water barrier around the poles. I bought about thirty baby chicks from a Makeni hatchery and placed them in their new home. The next morning I visited the chicks. Most were dead. Driver ants had climbed the corner poles and killed the chickens. Four or five were still alive, but they were getting weaker.

I was probably the talk of the village—probably a fool of sorts. What was I to do with a few chicks and a couple of dozen or more dead? I buried the dead. A couple more chicks died later that day or the next. I gave the survivors to a young girl in the village. The survivors grew like gangbusters. They were the girl's pride and put all the local chicks to shame. It was truly a hybrid fowl. Yes! I knew chickens!

11.

Saffie Daramy and Mammy Sallay

Saffie Daramy and Mammy Sallay were Makeni business partners. I thought they were sisters, but they might not have been. Both were quick, smart, hardworking entrepreneurs. They were also great dressers. They were proud. They were not ashamed of attention. They were great merrymakers. They were classy ladies. Many of us who knew them probably loved them.

I somehow knew Saffie better than Sallay. I thought Saffie's husband was a diamond miner, and as I recall was seldom in Makeni. Saffie had three daughters, Sallay—then known as Baby Sallay—Fatu, and Mabinty, and a son, Alpha.

Saffie and Mammy Sallay also raised Bassie Kamara, a young fellow who lived and worked with them. Saffie and Sallay were famous for garra cloth they tie-dyed and sold in lappas. Saffie and Sallay dyed their cloth in 55-gallon drums on the grounds of Sallay's house next to Makeni's central mosque. One could buy a lappa and have a tailor make a shirt for a man or buy two lappas for a two-piece dress for a woman. Some of us believed they made the best tie-dyed material in the country.

Saffie Daramy and Mammy Sallay at the 1967 wedding
of Peace Corps volunteers Gerry and Barbara Cashion in Makeni

They also ran a bar, which was across street from the mosque on Magburka Road. We PCVs knew the bar as "Saffie's." Next door to the bar was the home and shop of Momodu Kanneh, the wood and ivory carver. Some of my Peace Corps friends told me that Momodu had received recognition at New York's 1964 World's Fair for his work. Years later I tried to learn what Momodu might have displayed or what recognition he might have received at the African section of the fair. I have been unable to learn specifics.

Next door to Momodu's was the Makeni library, where I once borrowed *Life with Picasso*, a memoir by François Gilot, one of Picasso's

Mammy Sallay in Freetown in 2004

mistresses. I was surprised to find the book there, and I thoroughly enjoyed reading it. It motivated me to look at the world differently.

One day during my second year in the country Saffie asked me, "Pat, what are you bringing back to the US from Sierra Leone?"

"I don't really know," I said.

"How about some ivory?"

"Isn't ivory expensive? I'm not sure I can handle that."

She didn't pursue the issue with me, but in the end I suspected she entreated Momodu to make something for me. He did. He made a 3½ by 11¼-inch ivory carving of a woman and two children standing next

Saffie's former building and second-floor home in Makeni.
Ismael, Keh, and Ismael's brother stand in front of what was the bar area.

to a pineapple. I think the price of the carving was about 100 leones ($120).

We often lingered at Saffie's when we were in Makeni. The Peace Corps rest house on Daramy Street was half a block away. Saffie's was not fancy; at that time there was not much in Makeni one might call upscale. For most of Makeni's residents, life was hard, and over time it got worse. Saffie's was a bare-bones, two-story cement storefront with two steel roll-up doors facing Magburka Road. Saffie lived above the bar. Entry to Saffie's living quarters was by an open-air, un-railed stairway on an outside wall of the building. Her first-floor back-door porch overlooked a small area of palm trees, cassava plants, and in the rainy season a rice patch between her porch and the back-door cooking area of a neighbor's cement block house. Over time Saffie thought it boorish for some us to stand at her back porch and urinate into the open area rather than walk the half block to the Peace Corps rest house to relieve ourselves. At least once she persuaded me to use her facilities; they were not fancy—a hole in the floor with no stool.

The bar area was on one side of her storefront. On the other side she stored supplies. Late at night one could hear rats scurrying in the wall between the two areas. She sold Star Beer, Heineken, Guinness Stout, Diamond Gin, Parrot Tonic Water, and sometimes brandy and Scotch—Johnny Walker Red. She also sold cigarettes from the Aureole Tobacco Company and Coca-Cola products: Fanta, Sprite, and Coke. Star was the cheaper beer: Heineken and Guinness were dearer: a Star was 2 shillings (20 cents), and a Heineken or Guinness 2 shillings and 5 pence (25 cents).

None of us had much money, or so we thought, but in the grand scheme of things we must have had been well-to-do. The average per capita income in 1967 was about Le100 per year. My living allowance was Le120 per month. I lived in a village a few miles away and paid Foday 12 leones a month for laundry, cleaning, and watching the house when I was away. Other than food, transportation, beer, and garra cloth, I didn't have a lot of overhead to worry or even think about.

Saffie, Mammy Sallay, or Bassie tended the bar. Their trust in us was such that over time they would often go to bed and let us drink ourselves into the night before the PCVs returned to their Makeni home or the rest of us went to the PC rest house half a block away. Eventually we'd leave shillings or leones in the cigar box behind the counter to pay for the beer we had drunk, pull down the sliding door, lock up, and leave.

Some of us must have drunk a lot; we didn't seem to do much else. Some expatriates seemed to wallow in sex, alcohol, food, or other diversions—sometimes constructive, sometimes not. There was probably some drug use by a few PCVs while I was in Sierra Leone, but drugs of some type became a bigger issue for some PCVs in later years.

Saffie's was a place to hang out, to BS, to hear local palaver, and to recuperate from whatever our lives were like by ourselves in our postings. It was a pleasant place to do not much of anything but begin to re-emerge into a different reality. At least twice a few of us drank through the night and into the morning, late or early enough to watch and listen to the mosque's muezzin call worshipers to prayer. In our forced but usually pleasant friendly way of deciding who was paying for the next beer, no one seemed to get very belligerent, even when one or more of us had twelve Star beers once or twice. We were young, dumb, mostly healthy, energetic, and oblivious to much of the rest of the world.

After I had been in Sierra Leone more than a year I decided to vacation in Liberia to visit a Peace Corps friend. While sitting at the bar I peered over my Star beer and mentioned my upcoming trip to Saffie.

"Saffie, I'm going to Liberia to visit a friend. I'll bring you back a gift. What would you like?"

"Oh Pat, bring me back some brassieres. You can get American bras in Monrovia. I can only get British bras in Freetown. The American bras are much better."

I was young and more naïve than one might think. With a mother and five sisters, I knew what bras were and their purpose, but my experience with them was limited. I had taken bras to and from the clothesline, but I had never taken one to or from anyone or anything else.

"Sure, Saffie. What size do you want?"

"36D—a red one and a black one."

In Monrovia I ventured into an Indian merchant's shop, approached a display case, and bravely and directly peered through the glass. I pointed to the merchandise.

"I'll take one of those and one of those."

I purchased two bras, size 36D, one red, one black.

I returned to Makeni.

"Here's your gift, Saffie." I dropped the package on the bar and went merrily on my way.

A few days later a fellow PCV stayed at my home while he was traveling to Freetown. He mentioned he had been at Saffie's and she was really happy.

"I was at Saffie's, and she said, 'Look at what Pat brought me from

Monrovia.' She reached down to the hemline of her blouse, lifted the bodice over her head, and said, 'Look, isn't it wonderful?'"

I was happy that Saffie was pleased with the gift, but I do not remember if she ever commented to me about it. Some of us had seen her use her bra to hold cash. Whatever relationship we had, it was an uncomplicated one. I suspect she was closer to other Peace Corps personnel. She was a wonderful, inspirational woman. I sent her one letter after I returned to the US and connected with her son, Alpha, in 2004.

Saffie died in 1993. In 2004 her daughters Sallay and Fatu were living in Freetown. Mabinty had lived in the US for a long time but later returned to Sierra Leone and became the Sierra Leone government's Deputy of Trade and Industry. She became the Deputy Minister of Finance in 2013 and the Acting Minister of Trade and Industry in 2015, and she was named Sierra Leone's Ambassador to Guinea in 2016. In 2004 I gave Alpha copies of a photo I had taken of Saffie and Mammy Sallay at a Makeni Peace Corps couple's wedding in 1967. I also sent a copy of the photo to Mabinty when she was living in the United States. Prior to my 2004 visit I had heard that Mammy Sallay was blind. When I met with her in 2004, she was living in Freetown; she was not blind, but she had a bad hip.

In 2012 Alpha caught me up on news of Saffie's family. Saffie's Makeni home had been sold to a Fullah man who lived there with his family. Baby Sallay and Fatu were married and living in Freetown. Mammy Sallay had returned to her home in Makeni by then.

Baby Sallay had four children, all girls; three were married. The single daughter was living in the United States. Another was living in Freetown, married to an Afro-Lebanese man, and had two children. The third lived with her husband, a footballer, in Cyprus; they had two boys. The fourth daughter, Fatu, and her husband were living in Freetown and had two sons; one was living in France, and the other was living with Fatu and her husband and studying at a university.

Alpha was married, living in Freetown, and had three children, Ibrahim, Abu, and Alpha. Ibrahim was at university studying information technology. Abu had recently returned from the United States, was in politics, and was hoping to run for election. Alpha was in secondary school, Form 4.

Alpha, Saffie's son, in 2012 was a pensioner. He had been the General Manager of a branch of the Sierra Leone Commercial Bank Limited. He mentioned that except for Mabinty, he and two sisters each owned their Freetown homes, fully paid for—however Mabinty was "the only affluent amongst us." Alpha is an avid soccer fan.

~   ~   ~

Momodu Kanneh, the Makeni carver, died sometime before 2004, but his wife was living in Freetown. Two of his sons were now running the wood carving shop in Makeni. I bought a number of sandalwood carvings from them. One of them, Ismael, tracked me down in Freetown before I left, and I purchased two nomolis from him. Nomolis are soapstone figures that were originally buried in the

Ismael Kanneh (left), one of his brothers, and the carving staff
at the Makeni shop of Ismael's father, Momodu Kanneh

ground by the Mende people to protect their crops. During my earlier tour in the country as a PCV, nomolis were seemingly sacred figurines, and I believed they were generally unobtainable. I was surprised to find nomolis in Makeni, since the Mende people generally live in the south. How the figurines got to Makeni I did not have the time to pursue with Ismael.

Fatmata's garra cloth shop near the Makeni roundabout

The war devastated Makeni's garra cloth industry. In 2002 former PCVs, including me, worked with Africare staff member Alan Alemian, my former Northern Province Peace Corps director, who helped develop a micro-loan program to re-establish the industry in Makeni. On the Sunday morning before I left Makeni to return to Freetown in 2004, I purchased two lappas from a woman who had a stall near the central roundabout. The pieces cost Le20,000, about $7 apiece. She likely benefited from our efforts to revive the industry. Later, walking down a Freetown street, I mentioned to my guide, Keh (see page 96), that I wanted to have a shirt made from one of the lappas. As we walked to Dura's home Keh noticed a friend of his, a tailor, walking near us. The tailor pulled a measuring tape from around his shoulders and measured me up. I gave the lappa to him and had a shirt four hours later—the cost: Le30,000, about $11. Returning to Minnesota I took the second lappa to a St. Paul tailor. She measured me up one side and down the other. About three weeks later I had a shirt—the cost: $95.

12.

Snake Bitten

A group of Sierra Leone PCVs were sitting around an open-air wood fire in an upcountry village somewhere in the provinces during the dry season. One of the men felt one bite in his leg and hip area. The leg became numb. Not knowing what had bitten him and having no anti–snake venom available, the group quickly consulted the local head man for advice.

The head man told the volunteer that a centipede or a snake might have bitten him; both were poisonous. The head man said that if the bite was from a centipede, the leg would hurt but the PCV would be well in the morning; if the bite was from a snake the PCV would likely be dead in the morning. The next morning the volunteer was alive. I was not a member of that group sitting around the open-air wood fire camp.

~ ~ ~

When I was at the 2002 National Peace Corps Association 40+1 celebration in Washington, DC, former PCVs who had known of me but had not heard or seen me for years were at one time convinced I had been eaten by a snake while I was in Sierra Leone. I assured them I had not been. While living in Makeni during the 1968 rainy season I had been bitten by something, probably a snake, but did not know what kind.

Prior to going to West Africa I had never seriously looked into varieties of African snakes. My sense of snakes in general and African snakes in particular was that they were dangerous. I wanted to avoid them.

Peace Corps medical staff took snake bite precautions for volunteers, but their snake-bite preparations were not always on the mark. During the 2002 reunion a former Sierra Leone PCV I had known during my service told me a member of the Peace Corps medical staff had stored local anti–snake venom in her up-country refrigerator, but the venom was for snakes in North Africa and would have been worthless in Sierra Leone.

Prior to my snake-bite incident I met a PCV schoolteacher who lived in a village somewhere on the road between Makeni and Freetown and who had been bitten by a snake. With no anti–snake venom at hand he had gone to a neighbor for help. The local snakebite protocol involved "medicine" applied in three steps. The local man used three steps, but in the wrong order, and the teacher suffered the consequences. He walked with a limp, needed a cane, and had a huge black mark on his left foot and leg. He was alive, but suffering. He survived to continue teaching but was not as happy as I would be later when I encountered another snake.

When I had been in-country more than a year, I began to think of what memorabilia I might bring back to the US. One afternoon I was at Saffie's and saw a man walk by carrying two python skins, 10 to 12 feet in length. I ran to him and paid a few leones for them. I thought they would be interesting conversational items. I used them a number of times in school presentations; young kids have been enthralled. I eventually donated the skins to a St. Paul primary school.

Seeing snakes while I lived in Binkolo was not an everyday occurrence, but not unusual either. My encounters with live snakes were few, brief, and memorable. I had watched local schoolboys stone a green mamba slithering in a mango tree. The boys were excited, viciously aggressive, and efficient in their execution. It was easy to see terror and excitement in their faces and eyes as they energetically carried out their task.

Once, alone, riding a small motor bike, I encountered a green mamba slithering 20 to 30 yards ahead of me across a seldom traveled bush road in the chiefdom. The mamba felt earth tremors from the movement of the motorbike. Frightened, the 6- to 7-foot snake leaped into the air, head up, tail straight down and rushed into the bush when it hit the ground. It was astonishingly quick, and something I knew I did not want to mess with.

Later that dry season I was walking a chiefdom bush path from one village to another. I heard a rustle in the short, dry grass nearby. I paused and saw 6 to 8 inches of a fat, large something in the weeds. It was a snake—a python. I stopped, but not for long. The python did not want to be bothered with me, and I did want to be bothered with it.

After my eviction from Binkolo I moved into Makeni and lived alone in a house a quarter mile from the more populated areas of the town. One evening I planned to see a movie at the local cinema with a fellow Tanzania XIII PCV. He had traveled in from his posting in Mabang to buy supplies. It was sometime during the rainy season. I was to meet him at Saffie's about 6:30 and then go to the 7:00 movie. Both of us had been in-country more than twenty months, and our brains were partially fried and likely going even more haywire; almost any diversion was welcome. Whatever romantic ideas we might have had about what we came to do or had been doing were wearing thin.

I left my home in the dark wearing cut-off white shorts, a garra cloth shirt, and sandals. I probably was not wearing underwear. During the humid rainy season I seldom wore underwear to minimize heat rash in my groin area.

I had not walked far on the dirt road when I felt a bite on the inside of my right heel. I carried no flashlight. In my naïveté or complete innocence I had never gotten around to purchasing a flashlight for walking at night in Binkolo or anywhere else. No one I knew in

Binkolo seemed to have a flashlight, so why should I have one? In hindsight, having more than once earlier walked the hill to and from my Binkolo home, in complete darkness, during the rainy season, I had likely been a fortunate and foolish porto (white person).

I hoped I had not been not bitten by a snake. I hadn't heard or seen anything unusual. I continued walking. I told myself it was probably a scorpion sting, even though I didn't recall ever having seen a scorpion while in Sierra Leone. I wanted to believe I had nothing to worry about. After my earlier encounters with mambas and pythons, and having been fortunate to either scoot out of their way or have them scoot out of mine, I wanted to believe my good fortune would continue. Continuing to deny whatever sense of reality was left to my being I continued walking into town.

When I arrived at Saffie's I purchased a Star beer, sat down, and waited for my friend. Makeni then had electricity—there were lights in the bar. I could see two small marks on the inside of my heel. I wanted to believe the marks were of little concern. I wanted to believe the marks were scorpion stings even though they looked very much like snake fang marks. Undaunted, I continued to be a blithe spirit; I didn't feel anything unusual yet.

My PCV friend, who was staying not far away at the Makeni Peace Corps Rest House, walked into Saffie's, ordered a beer, and sat down with a cigarette.

"I think I've been bitten by a snake. Look at these marks," I said.

"Shit, Patrick, this doesn't look good. You'd better take care of that. I wonder where our supervisor is."

"Oh, he'll be around later, and I'll probably be all right. Anyway, we are going to the movie."

"Patrick, I wouldn't mess with a snake bite. A mamba bit a guy in a village near me, and he was a goner real quick. I wouldn't fuck around with a snake bite. The hospital is nearby—let's stop there on the way to the movie."

I still felt OK.

We walked to the hospital a couple of blocks away. A crowd had gathered at the dispensary door of Doctor Cole. Lactating women with babies wrapped to their backs and other women with ill children were trying to get Cole's attention.

My friend and I were the only portos—white people—seeking help at that time of the night from the dispenser.

My friend approached Dr. Cole's half-open Dutch door. The doctor was focusing on the needs of anxious women and children.

My friend did not have any success in attracting Cole's attention, even when he yelled, "I say! A snake has bitten my friend. He needs help!" Dr. Cole continued his duties. The women and children had their own issues, and Cole was not to be distracted by two PCVs who may or may not have known what they were doing in the country in the first place. From his point of view, we likely looked healthier than anyone else at his door; also, we likely had access to other medical services if either of us was in serious trouble.

My friend became more irritated. He began to loudly complain about what a lousy place the town was, how lousy the country was, and how piss-poor the people were. After all this time in Sierra Leone, both of us were likely emotionally exhausted from stress, isolation, loneliness, and other assorted psychoses, real and imagined. After my being evicted from Binkolo on very short notice, I did not want another fuss.

"Let's get out of here. The movie will start soon!" I pulled him away. We walked the short distance to the cinema.

We purchased tickets, beers, went in, and sat on the steel chairs in the auditorium. The cinema showed movie shorts followed by an intermission to enable patrons to purchase more snacks and refreshments prior to the start of the feature. As we sat and watched the movie shorts, my right leg began to swell and become numb. At intermission we rose to go for more refreshments, I could only stand on one leg. I could not walk by myself to the vestibule.

Not knowing what to do, but knowing we needed help, we hoped our supervisor would be at Saffie's by now. My friend carried me piggy back to Saffie's, where the supervisor was having a Star beer. I was soon lifted into his green Jeep pickup and driven to his home. A Dutch nurse, from St. Francis Teacher's College, was contacted and brought to the house. My heel and fang marks were examined by the nurse, her husband, and the rest of us. No one could decide what had bitten me. The group decided to treat it as a bite of the most potent of snakes we knew of in Sierra Leone, the Gabon viper. The nurse shot the first of four 10-cc vials into my butt as I lay on a goatskin rug in the middle of the living room floor. She pulled down the right corner of my white shorts for each of them. I had a huge mass of liquid, like a giant boil, near the top of my right derriere.

I was later lifted into the supervisor's vehicle, and the two of us drove to Freetown. The government had declared another state of emergency, and we encountered numerous police and army check points on our journey. We arrived at the home of Joe Kennedy, the Sierra Leone Peace Corps Director, at 4:00 AM. I was soon transferred to Connaught Hospital for two nights of observation. When I was released, I visited Dr. Gorman, the Peace Corps Doctor at his Free-town office. Gorman examined me and told me to clean up and return to my home. I hadn't shaved for a couple of days and was wearing the clothing I had worn to the cinema. I must have looked a bit rough.

A few months later my supervisor drove over a Gabon viper. He stopped to inspect the carcass. The snake was about 3 feet long and as wide as a car tire. Its head was the size of a fist and had fangs 2 inches long and 3 inches apart. Gabon vipers rarely attack humans, but if one does, the person normally dies in about fifteen minutes. Whatever had bitten me, I was fortunate.

13.

Land of Iron and Diamonds

When I first came to Sierra Leone in 1967 many Sierra Leone postage stamps were embossed with "The Land of Iron and Diamonds." My knowledge of the country was abysmal prior to arriving. The first time I became seriously aware of diamonds in the country was during our nine-week orientation tour, which included a few days in and near Kenema, the capital of Eastern Province, a diamond trading center not far from the diamond area. I have memories, possibly real, maybe not, of seeing of a pile of diamonds in a dealer's office. The office was a four-walled room inside his house with locks, a safe, and high-impact lighting for inspecting, grading, and purchasing any diamond prior to a later sale or smuggling out of the country.

The center of the diamond industry was in the Koidu-Sefadu area. At the time the area had a reputation of a Wild West, cowboy mentality. Years later I learned of an American from the Upper Midwest who had gone to Sierra Leone intending to get involved with diamond smuggling. Somewhere during his journey in or near the diamond area his vehicle was stopped by men bearing rifles and submachine guns. One man pointed his weapon through a car window seeking money.

The American later knew he was fortunate to get out of the country alive and eventually return to the Upper Midwest.

I visited the diamond mining area during the post-Christmas holidays in January 1968. I was a guest and traveling companion of Chief Dura and Pa Kiester, a Makeni merchant. We did not ride in Dura's Mercedes but in a Peugeot taxi from Makeni to the diamond area. Dura, Pa Kiester, or the driver played West African highlife music in the car much of the trip.

The military government still ruled, and soldiers manned numerous roadblocks to inspect riders and vehicles going to and coming from Sefadu, partially to try to thwart the smuggling of diamonds. While in the mining area we stayed at the home of a Limba diamond miner and trader. He had been fortunate. He was driving a new white Mercedes-Benz 230-S. His house was full of many schoolboys, presumably relatives, who had come to the area during holiday to work for school fees. In the African tradition a "big man" was expected to help or provide for relatives and the extended family.

Sierra Leone diamonds are in alluvial deposits not deep in the soil. Alluvial deposits are created by the erosion of kimberlite, a volcanic rock. The residue can be carried over wide areas by river systems. Alluvial diamond mining involves separating rough diamonds from earth and gravel by working with a sieve or large dredges. Much of Sefadu was pockmarked with open areas that had been mined and then abandoned in the midst of businesses and private homes seemingly randomly scattered among open spaces and semi-bush areas.

One evening Dura, Kiester, and I visited a Lebanese diamond dealer. The dealer lived in a large three-story rectangular cement unit across from a large pockmarked area in the town. The neighborhood was surrounded by a multitude of dug-out areas. The Lebanese man asked me what I was doing in the country. I briefly described my work with chiefdom farmers. I commented on the irony of my work and efforts at a time when the per-capita income may have been 100 leones a year and how someone with good fortune might become quite rich with a few diamond findings. Later a fellow PCV mentioned having been speaking to one of his chiefdom neighbors who had been a miner.

The neighbor told of crawling on his stomach with his forearms and elbows during the night "to sneak" away with whatever stones he had managed to find and hide during his work.

A couple of days later we motored to a diamond mining riverbank and village in our host's Mercedes. The road was terrible, even more difficult than most of the ones I was used to by then. Midway in our journey we passed a village where a local miner must have been very successful. Seemingly in the middle of nowhere someone had built a huge mosque to give thanks to Allah.

We eventually reached a riverbank and rode a small boat to a large ramshackle village of mud and bush-pole buildings with rusty zinc pan roofs. Along the riverbanks were men knee and waist deep in mud and water, digging and panning for diamonds. As we walked to the village center I saw a Russian magazine similar to the American magazines *Life* or *Look* lying on a table in a porch of one of the houses we walked past. I do not know if Russians were in the area. The only contact I can remember having with Russians while in Sierra Leone was during my second year, when I had a chest X-ray for a Peace Corps–mandated physical.

On our last night in Sefadu, Dura and Kiester held a meeting with a dozen or more men, presumably Limba. The 1967 coup d'état had intensified tribal issues between the north and south in ways I did not then comprehend. That was the only time I heard Dura voice true animosity toward other peoples in the country. Leading the conversation, he emphatically used the first two fingers on his right hand to slap his left arm as he stated that the peoples of the north must get even with the peoples of the south when the opportunity arose.

We returned to Makeni and Binkolo the next day. It was a great trip. I had been to parts of the country I had not visited before. I had traveled to places few PCVs were fortunate to have access to in the way I had. In light of the turmoil, which later increased, ripping and destroying the country in so many ways, the limited understanding I had of what I saw and heard at that last night's meeting was important. Over time the animosity I heard Dura mention metastasized again and again in ways I had not thought possible. Many years later Dura's daughter Jane, living in New Jersey, told me how upset her father was when she donated one of her kidneys to a Sierra Leonean woman who was not of the Limba people.

In 2004, when I mentioned the trip to Dura, he smiled and said, "Oh yes. Our reconnaissance trip." I was not with him long enough during that visit to gain more insight into what he meant then or so many years earlier.

14.

Peace Corps Service, Selective Service

While I was in Sierra Leone I met a number of male PCVs and became increasingly aware of the different behaviors of Selective Service draft boards regarding PCVs. A few PCVs believed we had an obligation to serve in the military at the end of our Peace Corps service. Others were groping for a different point of view, as the Vietnam War continued to escalate. Some draft boards seemed to consider Peace Corps service to be sufficient service. Other boards seemed to look at registrants as draft dodgers, but allowed volunteers to delay dealing with the draft issue until returning to the US. I believe I heard of one Sierra Leone PCV from somewhere in California who had to fly from Sierra Leone to a US military base in Europe for a draft physical. If that actually happened, I don't know who paid the airfare. At the time I thought the notice was onerous and capricious on the part of that draft board. However, after thinking of the parasites and other odd diseases all of us were either exposed to, might have been carrying, or were inoculated against, as well as the "normal malaria bout" many experienced while serving in West Africa, he might have been fortunate.

When I completed my Peace Corps service I returned to Minnesota and requested an interview with my local draft board early in 1969 to try to learn what I could expect for my future. By then, having been out of the US and in West Africa for two years, I had been exposed to enough turmoil in many parts of the world to believe that, at minimum, the US military involvement in Vietnam was a serious mistake and not worth supporting by enlisting or accepting being drafted. After the interview I received classification 1-A, "available for unrestricted military service"—draftable—and later underwent a physical exam at the Armed Forces Entrance and Examination Station in Minneapolis. During this period I submitted a request to my local Selective Service board for 1-O, conscientious objector status. It was turned down. When I submitted my request and supporting material I was employed at Minneapolis' St. Barnabas Hospital in the mental health ward and hoped to have my employment substitute for two years of military service.

I later received a Notice of Induction ordering me to report at the Armed Forces Entrance and Examination Station to enter the military. I reported to the station with the intent to refuse to comply with the induction ceremony.

I completed initial screenings but somehow was not included in a group sent to the induction room. Through a mix-up of some kind, I spent the remainder of my time chatting with two young military personnel at the main entrance. They eventually told me I was free to go home; they could see no reason for me to hang around. A day or two later I received a phone call from a Minneapolis/St. Paul FBI agent accusing me of "absconding the induction center." I informed the agent that I had reported to the center with the intent to refuse induction but was eventually told to leave the building. In the spring of 1970 I received another induction notice; I appeared, and refused induction.

~   ~   ~

In the spring of 1969 I began attending school at the University of Minnesota in Minneapolis and somehow met a number of students who had also been PCVs. One of them had mentioned my name to another former PCV, saying, "You got to meet this guy. He is still really out there."

A few were members of the local chapter of the Committee of Returned Volunteers (CRV), primarily former PCVs. One of the Minnesota members was very active with the national CRV group and the 1968 anti-war march on Washington. In the fall of 1969 the Minnesota chapter hosted a national CRV meeting at a church camp near St. Paul. One attendee at the meeting was a Jeff Jones, who wasn't a former PCV but was active in an anti-war group called the Weathermen. Jones attended the St. Paul meeting to encourage attendees to come to the October 1969 Days of Rage demonstration in Chicago during the Chicago Eight trial.

After the St. Paul meeting the Minneapolis FBI office contacted some members of the Minnesota CRV group and inquired of their attendance at the meeting, asking such questions as: Did you attend the meeting? What did you hear? What did you do? What would you do? Who was there? During that time the head of the Minneapolis/St. Paul FBI office was a man whose last name was Waller. The editor of our Minnesota CRV newsletter wrote an article called "Up Against the Waller" about this petty harassment, which went on for more than a year after the meeting.

I began working as a draft counselor for an organization called Minnesota Draft Help at the American Friends Service Committee office on 4th Street Southeast, near the Minneapolis campus of the University of Minnesota. I worked at Minnesota Draft Help until August of 1972.

During this time I had had hopes of a career with the US Foreign Service. I passed the initial written exam and went to Chicago for the oral interview. The interview may have been promising at first but took a real downturn when I candidly but badly told my story of having refused induction, and said that I was waiting to learn if I might be prosecuted. I failed the interview, and my hopes of a Foreign Service career disappeared.

Then, one Thursday in September 1971, Minnesota's US attorney indicted more than 150 Minnesota men for Selective Service violations. The next day we at the American Friends Service Committee contacted the US attorney's office to check on the names of the men indicted, seeking any information we could get on young men with whom we had been working. The name Patrick R. O'Leary, my name, was on the list. I returned home to my wife upset, shaken, and devastated, not knowing what to do. On Saturday I received a letter from my Albert Lea draft board informing me that the Minnesota US attorney's office had reviewed my file and found no grounds for prosecution. By now I was twenty-seven years old—too old to be drafted. The following Monday I learned that the indicted Patrick R. O'Leary lived in Minneapolis. I lived in St. Paul.

In 1972 I entered the master's program at the Atlanta University School of Social Work, founded in 1920—the oldest historically black school of social work in the world. I knew most of the students would be African Americans. Over time I eventually thought the school was likely receiving federal monies and needed some minority students— white students. Given the state of race relations in the US at that time, most white students interested in the social work field might have had a difficult time remaining in the school. I was likely a good bet to be able to stay with the program. Other than my aptitude scores, I thought the school knew little about me. I visited Atlanta to seek housing for my spouse and me. Staff at the school greeted me as "Rev. O'Leary," undoubtedly after a cursory review of my application and knowledge of my three years of study at a seminary in Minnesota.

Atlanta was a two-year program: two semesters of classes, one semester of work placement, and a final semester of classes. My more than sixty classmates were mostly African Americans, but at least five that I can remember were not black. There was also a Toronto man originally from Jamaica and a young man from India. Our class was separated into four colloquiums that served as core learning and support groups as we journeyed through the program. The colloquiums enabled us to gain insight into the school's program and into ourselves.

During graduate school I was again living as a minority and consciously and subconsciously learning much about an America I had not grown up with or experienced in my travels. Living as a minority again could be stressful, but I was able to work off much of the anxiety I might have developed by living 8 miles away from the campus and biking back and forth most days.

Adjusting to the environment of being a minority again was a new learning curve. An early dilemma occurred shortly into the new school year. The school held a weekend evening get-together for our incoming class and the faculty at the Dean's residence. I and a faculty member, who had apparently worked with many publications, got into a long argument about social policy issues and social workers. After the party we drove the faculty member to an after-hours establishment, where he purchased more liquor. Eventually our argument got visceral. As we eventually parted he brazenly told me I would never graduate from the school. The following Monday morning we encountered each other entering the administration headquarters. He approached and said that whatever had happened between us "never happened" and there would be no further issues between us. I was uncomfortable with the issue and wondered if the story was really finished. Whether his statement was on the mark or not I never needed to find out. The following Thanksgiving weekend holiday he journeyed to Harlem in New York City and died of a heart attack.

~   ~   ~

After the first year of school I had an internship at a Georgia Department of Human Services methadone clinic on 10th Street in Atlanta. During staff introductions a woman stated she had graduated from "a radical school in the North." Intrigued, I asked what she meant by "a radical school." My impression of her didn't suggest a radical persona. "The University of Wisconsin, Madison," she said. I was amused and befuddled; I must have been away for so long I did not begin to understand or appreciate how or what "radical" might have meant to some.

One day the pharmacy nurse staffing the clinic was unavailable. The temporary replacement, the agency's head nurse, was curt and hostile when a male patient approached the pharmacy counter for methadone. "It's not ready yet! Sit down!" she yelled, slamming the pharmacy's glass window and returning to her preparations.

"You bitch!" the patient yelled as he stepped away from the counter and drew a small silver pistol from his pocket. I had been sitting close-by in the clinic's waiting area and had begun to rise to intervene when the yelling started. I was not yet standing when the pistol appeared. Silently and slowly I eased back into my chair as the guy cursed, muttered, and waived the pistol in the air. He quickly left the clinic but returned later and received his methadone seemingly with no repercussions. Later, around holiday time, during a colloquium session discussion about the black family, a female classmate from Tennessee mentioned that she kept a pistol on her car seat when she drove home for the holidays. Another time she casually mentioned, "I know a man loves me when he beats me." This was the first time I had heard such comments.

Another female classmate more than once described her fear and anger when, on May 14–15, 1970, at Jackson State University in Jackson, Mississippi, National Guard and state police fired at her women's dormitory. Two students were killed, twelve others struck by gunfire. A few days earlier, on May 4, at Kent State University in Kent, Ohio, four students were shot and killed and nine others were wounded when the National Guard shot at students protesting the invasion of Cambodia by US troops.

In 1965 the US Department of Labor published *The Negro Family: The Case for National Action*, often referred to as the "Moynihan Report" after its main author, Daniel Patrick Moynihan. Some of the school's faculty read the report as an attack on African American morality, and at times some of the faculty were not shy in supporting such an analysis of black and white issues and encouraged a like opinion.

Such teaching at times led to a milder colloquium discussion of race relations, such as comments between a fair-skinned mixed-race single woman from Washington, DC, and the Indian man. The man was married to a woman from India, but at times he seemed fond of the woman from Washington. She seemed to enjoy some of his attention, but from time to time was annoyed with some of his other behavior. Once, she clearly didn't care for a remark he made during a session on the black family. She emphatically stated to him, "You are so confused you don't know if you are black or white."

During another black family session there was much discussion of "Negro this" or "Negro that." One of my classmates was puzzled and confronted me with whatever I had said and how I said the word "Negro."

"What did you say? Pat, did you say NIgro or NEEgro?" I have forgotten my response, but whatever it was it startled her. She continued, "Pat, you're different, and that bothers me." I had left much of what I had earlier been exposed to as a youth in southern Minnesota.

~   ~   ~

In October 2000 I returned to Atlanta for the eightieth anniversary celebration for the School of Social Work. My new wife of two years accompanied me. It was her first visit to Atlanta. I had told her I had attended "a mostly black school." She thought she knew what that meant.

We returned to the campus I had left so long ago. It took me a while to get my bearings. There had been a major infusion of federal funds during the Clinton administration; parts of the campus had changed and been built up.

We parked our car and walked through the campus. After a few minutes she grabbed my hand and said, "What is this? There aren't any white people here!"

"Sure there are. I've seen three others," I said.

"It must have been difficult here," she said. At times it was.

Whatever I had brought back from Sierra Leone, my journeys and maturation made it easier to survive the many difficulties and surprises of my time and studies in Atlanta. Somehow I had developed a sense of myself other than the one I had had at an earlier time. I was then, and was even more so now, becoming someone else. Either by accident or by design I did not follow the Freeborn County nurse's 1966 admonition to not "bring one back." I brought back much more.

15.

"This Country Has Been Ruined"

The mail I had sent to Chief Dura in 1996 was returned due to "temporarily suspended" mail service during the war, which prevented further contact with him. My membership and involvement with the Friends of Sierra Leone (FOSL), made up primarily of former US PCVs and Sierra Leone expatriates kept me partially involved in the country. I had been distantly aware of the turmoil and personalities that gradually developed in the country, but I was unable to understand and appreciate either the level of disintegration or any motivation or intentions of the personnel in the country.

In the 1990s my only direct knowledge of what might be happening in the country was from one of my brothers, a Washington, DC, immigration attorney. Many of his clients were from Sierra Leone, seeking asylum in the United States. At least one was a wife of former president Joseph Saidu Momoh, who had been exiled in Guinea. During this period my brother showed me photos provided by refugees seeking asylum. One photo was of five men in a village, one of the men holding a severed head in his hands as if it was a basketball. Another was of a young male sitting on the ground holding a rifle, surrounded by ten severed heads. During this period I somehow came across a color photo on the Internet of a twelve-year-old girl, eyes burnt out, raped, and murdered.

After I first left Sierra Leone I read a number of books about many parts of Africa. Among them was *Journey Without Maps*, Graham Greene's account of his 1936 overland trip from Freetown to Liberia. I was originally amused by Greene's description of inspecting a map in a Freetown office and seeing the region beyond Bo, a city in Sierra Leone's eastern area, described as "unexplored territory, cannibals." I had been in Bo a few times during my PC service and thought Greene's depiction indicated simple ignorance or colonial prejudices. However, my later knowledge of rebel war behavior—which often included murder, body dismembering, and sometimes removal of a victim's heart and cooking and eating it to gain courage—moved some of my earlier thoughts to a completely different realm. Returning to Sierra Leone years later and seeing the wantonly desecrated bodies, severed and mangled limbs, severely damaged buildings, and piles of garbage in the street reinforced my bewilderment with the new reality.

Being unable to contact Chief Dura I searched the Internet. These searches listed him as Paramount Chief of the chiefdom, so I believed he might still be alive. I had no sense of the reliability of the Internet references until Dura's existence was eventually confirmed to me by Alan Alemian, my former Sierra Leone Peace Corps supervisor, who had been working with Africare. In 1998 he had seen Dura in Freetown; he believed Dura had moved to London, was in ill health, and might be blind.

When the Friends of Sierra Leone announced it would hold its June 2004 annual meeting in Freetown I contacted the organization and decided to join the group going to the meeting. I also increased efforts to locate Dura.

With hard work and luck I obtained a Freetown phone number for him. I phoned. He recognized my name and voice almost immediately. His first words me were "Pat, this country has been ruined." I told him I was coming to Sierra Leone on Ghana Airways and hoped to see him. "Don't fly them. They are thieves! They are always late and never leave when they are scheduled. Fly Sabena from Brussels or British Airways."

I was invigorated, but apprehensive about my return. A few days prior to leaving Minnesota I noticed a newspaper article telling about an American, John Auffrey, who had once worked for the Peace Corps in Sierra Leone and had been working for the US Department of Defense in Monrovia, Liberia, assessing the establishment of a new Liberian army. In May 2004, while staying at Monrovia's Mamba Point Hotel, men entered Auffrey's room through a false ceiling after breaking into a room next door, stole $8,000, and killed him. I did not share that story with my wife, who was not accompanying me; she was worried enough about my journey based on whatever she thought she knew about West Africa.

The Chief was partially right. My initial itinerary called for a seven-hour layover in Accra, Ghana, with a connecting flight to Freetown. The layover became thirty hours. Medical personnel of some sort commandeered our scheduled flight to deliver emergency medical supplies and personnel to Monrovia. The plane later flew to Nigeria before returning to Accra, and by then was leaking fluids. The pilots refused to continue flying. We eventually obtained visas to enter Accra and stay at the Kumbaya Hotel, which the airline booked for us. Even though we arrived a day later than expected, we were fortunate. Not long after I returned to the US, some Ghana Airways passengers in Accra became so upset with unexpected delays that they kidnapped the plane's pilots. Incidents such as these can seem comic from a distance but are excruciating to endure. In July 2004 the US government banned Ghana Airways from flying into the United States. The ban has yet to be lifted.

~   ~   ~

During our phone call I had asked Chief Dura if he would recommend a place for me to stay during my visit. He did, and said he would have someone meet me at the airport. I was met at Lungi, Freetown's airport, by Peter Dura, a son of the Chief, and Mohamed Keh Banya, a thirty-four-year-old man Chief Dura had assigned to be with me during my visit. Keh, unmarried, had a twelve-year-old daughter and had been unemployed (he used the term "redundant") for six years. During the troubles he had been jailed—he was to be killed—until an authority recognized him and had him released. Keh had chronic symptoms of low-level malaria during the entire time we were together.

Mohamed Keh Banya and me
in the ferry as I am returning to Lungi Airport

~ ~ ~

As our plane landed and taxied to Lungi's terminal evidence of the recent war was very apparent. Signs of the United Nations' Mission in Sierra Leone (UNAMSIL), then the largest UN peacekeeping force yet deployed anywhere, bordered the runway: UN helicopters, bunkers, and personnel armed with machine guns. We disembarked and, approaching the terminal were confronted with a billboard: "Wel-

come to Sierra Leone. If you cannot help us, please do not corrupt us."
In Freetown proper I later saw a billboard with a similar message: "Be
Patriotic. Report a Corrupt Practice Today."

I had been well prepared prior to my arrival. Alan, my former
Peace Corps supervisor, who had been in the country more recently,
recommended I change some currency at the airport. I seemed to be
the only member of the FOSL group to do so. Sierra Leone was now
a cash economy. During that visit, credit and ATM cards were of no
use. With a money pouch wrapped around my groin area, I eventually
realized I was a walking bank.

I didn't waste any time getting into the swing of things. Keh and I
took a taxi from the airport to the ferry for the one-hour ride across the
Sierra Leone River to reach Freetown. I was stunned by the generally
horrible living conditions I saw through the taxi windows as we rode
to the ferry. After being away for thirty-six years, almost everything
seemed to have backslid in huge ways.

A disheveled lady on the ferry was wearing a T-shirt with the
words "Who Wants to Be a Millionaire." I learned that surplus clothing donations from other parts of the world were commonly called
"junk." Having grown up with a lot of hand-me-down clothing, a few
pieces of which I still cherish in memory, I do not object to wearing
used clothing. But "junk" was a disincentive for the local economy
to generate more indigenous clothing. When I returned to the US I
got involved with a number of Kiva micro-loan programs in Sierra
Leone that enable people to borrow funds to start small businesses,
some involving purchasing boxes of used clothing and selling it piece
by piece.

Disembarking the ferry, Keh and I continued into Freetown in
another taxi. Most if not all of my FOSL colleagues seemed to take a
KTI Express Travel and Tours vehicle into town.

Dura had located sleeping accommodations for me not far from
his Freetown home. The three-story Place Guest House was secure,
clean, and centrally located, but unknown to any expatriates I met during my stay. The posted rate for my room was Le25,000. I was charged
Le30,000 (about $11) for each night I spent in the country whether I

The Place Guest House, 42 Rowden Street, Freetown

stayed in the room or not. Knowing I was in a place where most people lived on $1 a day or less, and having some sense of local customs, I did not quibble about the price and place the Chief had arranged for me.

Upon entering The Place, Hannah, the day desk clerk, showed me the room, a private suite, and asked, "Mr. Patrick, is this acceptable?" My only question was whether the shower worked. It did. The room was acceptable.

My lodging consisted of a room with a bed, a small closet, and a rickety chest of drawers, plus a private bath with a working toilet, a shower, a sink, and a towel, but no mirror. I soon realized the sink drained directly to the floor. There was no partition or curtain shielding the toilet from the shower area. Shower water ran to a hole in the ceramic tile baseboard below the sink.

The Place had electricity in the evening from 7:00 PM to 10:00 PM and in the morning at 5:30 for a couple of hours when a private generator was used.

Policies applicable to all guests were attached to the back of the room door: "All monies and valuables must be deposited with the General Manager for safe keeping. Maximum deposit must not exceed Le200,000. Do not use any room as an Office. Two adults of the same sex are not allowed to occupy the same room. No guest is allowed to bring more than one child into a room. YOU ARE WARNED BY THE MANAGEMENT."

I do not know how well the room policies were followed. I do know that the last night I stayed at The Place the room across the hall from me was used by three fellows.

~ ~ ~

Extensive war damage was evident in many parts of the city. A few steps from The Place was a large damaged church with no roof or windows; fire had gutted the interior. On a nearby street corner upper

Destroyed Freetown church half a block from The Place Guest House

floors of buildings were empty because of fire and war damage. Not far away, government buildings torched during the war were gradually being refurbished. The first two days I was at The Place a large pile of garbage lay at a street corner not far from our door.

Typhoid fever and other illnesses were claiming lives because Freetown's water supply, although filtered, was not chemically treated and was contaminated with *Salmonella*.

Electricity was available only from private generators, even though Freetown was expected to have electricity in 2008. A good day in Freetown was when phone, water, and electricity services worked at the same time.

A city of more than five hundred thousand people, Freetown had no stop signs. The male illiteracy rate in the country was 65 percent.

Even though the city and country was poor I was surprised to see a "poor box" for donations in the downtown St. George Cathedral.

~   ~   ~

There were other changes I noticed in Freetown. Walking a few blocks from The Place I came across a dozen men on their knees on the sidewalk, praying and bowing toward Mecca. In all my previous time and travel throughout the country I had never seen such public praying by Muslims in the country.

~   ~   ~

Shortly after arriving I had a lunch of millet, fish sauce, fresh mango, salad, and bottled water with the Chief at the Sackville Street home of Minnie, his Freetown wife. They had been married fifty-two years. I had met Minnie in 1968 when I took a taxi to her home to meet the Chief and ride in his Mercedes to the State House for the reopening Sierra Leone's parliament.

The Chief was indeed blind, but still vigorous. Jailed in 1996 and unable to obtain medicine for his eyes, his optic nerves froze. He told me that after his release he lived in London until September 2003. In 1997 Minnie moved to Atlanta, Georgia, to live with her sons Ahmed and Bimba. She returned to Sierra Leone in January 2004.

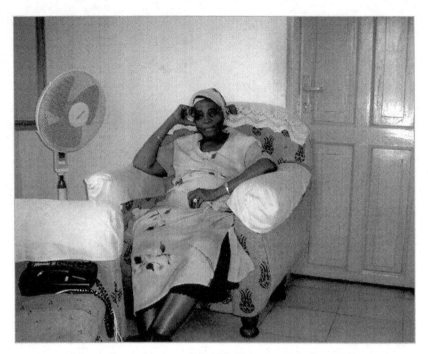

Minnie Dura, Alimamy Dura II's Freetown wife, June 2004

Minnie's Freetown home had been damaged by Nigerian artillery during the war, and it had yet to be completely repaired. Sackville Street was in rough shape. The pavement, and the garbage on the street, were such that no autos could drive on it. The remains of a burned-out automobile were a few steps from their door. Young boys played in the street with a rat on a string.

The situation in Binkolo was no better. The Chief told me that it had been a center of the war for a time in 1997. Many homes were destroyed or severely damaged. His village compound was burned. Papers he had retained in order to write his memoirs had been destroyed in the fires. A brother of Augusta, the youngest of Dura's wives, whom I had known, had assisted in the torching of the compound.

~   ~   ~

Many of the members of the FOSL group met a couple of days later at the US embassy for a security briefing. By then, with Keh's help, I had already done most of what was recommended to avoid, such as ride in public taxis with an unknown driver, eat food sold by street venders, and exchange money on the black market. The embassy personnel also told us that on a per capita basis Freetown had the highest number of Mercedes vehicles in the world.

~   ~   ~

Early during this visit I bought kola nuts from a Freetown street vendor. Kola nuts have a slightly bitter taste that suppresses hunger. They can also be a symbol of friendship that one might share with someone you meet. When I earlier came to the country I usually carried kola nuts in my shirt pocket and chewed on them as I walked bush paths to visit villages and farms. Back then I could buy three kola nuts for 1 cent. Now, in Freetown, the cost for five kola nuts was Le1,000. The cost of a bottle of Star Beer was now Le1,500, as compared to 20 shillings (cents) in 1967 for one. Inflation was astronomical.

~   ~   ~

Blue T-shirts printed with "Friends of Sierra Leone" and an outlined map of the country were worn by all of the attendees at the FOSL annual meeting, and the identification served us well. Later, wearing the shirt walking through town, it was common for Keh and me to be greeted with, "Peace Corps, Peace Corps. Are you coming back?"

One fellow approached me and told me we had met at Lumley Beach. I had not been there since 1968; his ploy is one often used to try to intimidate new visitors one way or another.

The interest in the Peace Corps reflected the tremendous need for skilled and semi-skilled personnel to assist with the nation's recovery from the horrible quagmire of war. The addition of new personnel could address some of those issues as well as bring increased cash into an economy that desperately needed it.

~   ~   ~

On our first night in-country, FOSL held a reception at China House, a conference center built by the Chinese government. During the event a FOSL member who had been a PCV about the same time as I had been approached me to exchange dollars for local currency—he had not done so at the airport. I had a bundle of local currency in a money pouch at my waist under my shorts. I moved to a back door stoop and was fumbling with the pouch when a female conference center employee approached and said, "Sir, if you need to ease, we have a place for that!"

~ ~ ~

A couple of days later Keh and I rode up country to Makeni in a fourteen-passenger vehicle with a driver and twenty-one passengers. I held a baby about a year old in my lap during most of the trip. We encountered four or five police checkpoints. At each stop the driver "dashed" cash (gave small bribes or gifts) to the police to enable us to continue on. Keh told me the driver paid Le50,000, about $20, during the trip as dashes. The reasons for the payments were unclear to me. I knew, though, that the government was trying to improve traveler safety. The driver may not have had proper papers, the vehicle may have simply been overloaded with passengers, or the payments may simply have been small bribes. Whatever the reason for the payments, we traveled to Makeni with no trouble.

In 2004 Makeni had no electricity without private generators. Running water was no longer available. Rebels had occupied the town for eight months late in the war, and the effects were still evident. Some home sites were still rubble. The last home where I had lived in Makeni had been destroyed by fire. The building was overgrown with weeds. The Choithrams grocery was gone, a distant memory. What had been the town library was an empty shell of a building with no roof or windows; it too had been torched. Next to what had been the Peace Corps rest house, the foundation of a house was now a garden of corn stalks. At that house I had periodically purchased what we called "Peace Corps sandals" for 2 shillings and 6 pence, or 25 cents. The effects of the war were horrendous.

My Makeni hotel was the most secure of the public accommodations available. At the Buya Hotel I again had a private suite with a bed, mosquito netting, a fan, a chair, a toilet, and a shower. I also rented lodging for Keh. After giving the clerk Le25,000 as a deposit, I returned to my room to freshen up after the ride. It was not yet dark. The hotel's electric generator had not yet started, the room was dim. I grabbed my flashlight, pointed the beam toward the shower head, and suddenly realized, "By God, there is no running water in this place."

The Buya's water was drawn from a private well with rope and a pail on the compound grounds. Each room was supplied with a 5-gallon pail of water for bathing and flushing the toilet. The Buya's cement brick compound walls were ringed with razor wire to keep away troublemakers. Some visitors might have been intimidated by the condition of the place. I was not. Having lived in the town years earlier, I was bothered by the growth and desolation of the city but not aware enough of the dismal reality to be intimidated by it. I still had memories of what once had been, even though much of it was no longer evident.

Years earlier Freetown and Makeni and other parts of the country had reliable electricity and running water. During this visit both cities had electricity only from private generators. In 2015 I learned that Makeni, by then a town of ninety thousand people, eventually received electricity after being without it for thirty-five years. Freetown has electricity again as well, but service is spotty.

In 2016 less than 12 percent of Sierra Leone cities had access to electricity, and in rural areas it was less 1 percent. The government is initiating a solar power project and hopes to bring electricity to all by 2025.

Africans indigenous to Sierra Leone and neighboring countries seemed to have had replaced many Lebanese and Indian shopkeepers in both Freetown and Makeni.

Some internal roads were very good; many were not. There was smuggling to and from Guinea and Liberia. An active mining industry, for iron ore and minerals, had been curtailed and waited for renewal. Diamonds were still being smuggled. During our FOSL meeting at

Freetown's China House, World Bank representatives told us government diamond revenue was 30 percent of what it should have been.

~   ~   ~

The next day I wanted to travel to Binkolo, where I had lived thirty-six years earlier. Keh and I walked to Makeni's lorry park to seek transportation. The lorry park I remembered as a place of friendly hubbub and gentle pandemonium was now an intense area of taxis, busses, and lorries, and an open-air space surrounded with three-walled, roofed stalls of marketers desperately trying to earn money by selling food, cloth, medicine, drink, gadgets, and whatever a transient might need. What I had remembered as a cheerful center of commercial opportunity had become a center of aggressive desperation.

Years earlier I and others traveling in public lorries had often purchased loaves of French-type breads and filled them with shish kebab meat, most likely beef, for snacks during our journey. Many of us called the meat "monkey meat." In light of the horrible deterioration of the health of the population, many of our casual PCV comments of years earlier took on an entirely new dimension.

Entering a place like Sierra Leone one should expect to be stunned in unexpected ways. The first person I encountered in the lorry park was a young boy holding a wooden stick leading a much older blind man begging for money. I next encountered an attractive, well-dressed dark-skinned young woman. She extended her right arm, begging for money. Her arm had been burned. I waved her away. She extended her left arm; the tendons of her wrist had been chopped with a machete. Her fingers were curled and mangled like a pile of rubber bands. I reached for a coin in my left pocket—and realized I had been pickpocketed. Fortunately I had two billfolds; the thief had gotten the smaller one. Most of my funds were somewhere else on my body. The losses, to me, were not drastic. I was fortunate but felt foolish and attacked.

Binkolo was changed. Arriving there I approached Dura's compound and met one of his sons, Momoh, and a man named Alpha, who had been a schoolboy when I lived in the village. Both remembered me. They were rebuilding Chief Dura's home. Alpha had remained in or around the village when rebels invaded in 1997. He spoke of weapons being hidden in the bush. He spoke of helicopter gunships, of machine guns, of rebels shedding military uniforms, of their raining carnage and raping village women.

I quickly learned there were no sleeping accommodations available in the village. For a brief time the village had been a point of contention during the war, and much had been pillaged; one third to one half or more of the homes had been destroyed. The village was still badly scarred. What once had been homes were now vegetable plots or remnants of destroyed walls. What had once been porches were now rubble from steps and pillars. Most people I had known were either dead or had fled the area. Five water wells with Japanese hand pumps had been added in the late 1980s. During this visit only one pump and well with potable water was working. Two wells were now dry. Rebels had damaged four of the other hand pumps.

~   ~   ~

Many conventional sources suggest that in Sierra Leone approximately 60 percent of the people are Muslim, 30 percent Christian, and 10 percent animist. That has been my supposition for years. Although I recently learned the reality might be different. My former PC supervisor told me of a Magburka secondary school principal speaking to a group of PCVs about religion in Sierra Leone once saying the people are 15 percent Christian, 15 percent Muslim, and 100 percent animist. I commented to Momoh that a tall cotton tree near Binkolo's village center was gone and asked what happened to it. Villagers had cut it down; "Too many evil spirits," he said.

There were now four churches in Binkolo: Apostolic, American Wesleyan, Muslim, and Roman Catholic. During my earlier time I remember no functioning village churches, but I do remember people walking to Mafari, a nearby village, for services led by a delightful-sounding fellow named Pa Mark. I never attended his services and have long regretted my failure to do so. The female Peace Corps teacher who was in Binkolo when I was attended at least one of the services and described it in this way: The service was held in Mafari's barre, a gazebo or similar structure, often with a grass roof in the open-air meeting place in the center of the village. Men and women sat in separate groups on narrow wooden benches. When the collection was held Mark would compare the gifts from one side with gifts of the other side. If there was a significant discrepancy in the gifts from one side, Mark would return to the other side for future consideration of the gifts.

There were now four school buildings in the village: a Roman Catholic primary school, an Islamic school, and empty remnants of what had been the government primary school and what had been Dura High School.

The 600-acre palm plantation started earlier was now capable of producing palm kernels and palm oil, although the trees needed to be pruned and areas around them needed to be cleaned to improve production. No funds were available to hire workers.

In 1987 Koreans began work on a hydroelectric project 11 miles away at Bumbuna Falls to provide power to parts of the country. Due to the war the project was abandoned in 1997 when the work was 85 percent completed. The dam was finally completed in 2009. During my 2004 visit I saw remnants of what would have been Binkolo's power relay station. The building had been burned, leaving a windowless, roofless shed near the path to the village cemetery. Binkolo installed street lights, likely solar powered, in 2015.

Indian representatives at one time had started negotiations with the Chief to open a stone quarry to make green, blue, pink, and white stone tiles. Chief Dura told me Binkolo was the only site in the country with stones of that nature. The war canceled whatever might have happened to the project.

During this visit Momoh and I went to the bridge site I had worked at years earlier. As we walked, a slight rain developed. We waited under a mango or orange tree for it to stop and talked about the recent NCAA basketball championship. Momoh had lived in the United States for twelve years, mostly in the New Jersey area, and worked in the health care industry. Momoh hoped to return to the United States. (See the photo on the following page.)

Momoh Dura, son of Alimamy Dura II,
with some of his family in Binkolo in 2004

Binkolo had prospered during the late '80s. Joseph Saidu Momoh, the president of Sierra Leone during that period, had been born in Mombokani, a village in Safroko Limba Chiefdom, and later made Binkolo his home village. He recruited many Binkolo and Limba natives to the military during his rule. Many of those who benefited from his influence built large homes in the village. Internet searches often referred to "the palaces of Binkolo." All of what might have been "palace" remnants had been destroyed.

President Momoh had built a huge compound atop a rocky mesa overlooking the village's primary school, Dura High School, the American Wesleyan Mission compound, and the countryside. An 8-foot-high cement block wall enclosed a large home, quarters for guards, and an outer building for other personnel. Outside the compound was a fenced tennis court—the site of the 1986 Sierra Leone National Tennis Championships.

The compound had been trashed. The roof, windows, and three air conditioners had been removed. The home's main wooden door was still on its hinges, but glass or plastic panels along the door frame had been removed. Dust and puddles of water and mud lingered on the building's tile floors. A 6-foot papaya plant grew on the tile floor of an uncovered porch and veranda area at the back of the living quarters.

My former village home was still being used, although it had been modified. The back door had been filled in, and a new door built on the north side of the building. The kitchen area had been enlarged; the porch was now smaller. A window had been added to the east side of the building. The house had been partitioned into smaller rooms, presumably to increase rental income. During my PCV tour I had been such a blithe spirit that I had never considered rental costs or thought of my home as rental property. My latrine and bathing area had been replaced by what had been a large house that was probably destroyed in 1997. All that remained of whatever had once been there was a couple of steps, debris and weeds, and a water pipe and faucet protruding from what remained of a foundation. Additional buildings had also been built near the destroyed home, but whatever had been built was in disarray, charred, overgrown, and returning to bush.

While I was inspecting the grounds around my former residence, a young man approached and asked who I was. I mentioned I had lived in this house years earlier and asked him where he lived. He said he lived in the brown mud block house down the hill where my neighbor Pa Tamba Kargbo had lived with his wives, Yenki and Yabu.

I looked down the hill through a cassava plant and mango and palm trees to a mud house that looked remarkably similar to the one that had been there years earlier. Through the undergrowth I saw a woman entering the back door of the house. I thought I recognized the way she moved. I walked down the hill to say hello. When I arrived at the back of the house, out came Pa Tamba. Pa Tamba was still alive! Pa Tamba was now the village medicine dispenser. We said "Kushe" to each other—"hello" in Krio. Suddenly, Yenki came to the open door from inside the house, saw me, and screamed, "Patrick!" She rushed to me, grabbed my waist, knelt on one knee, and bowed down to me.

Tamba and his family had fled the village during the war. Yenki was still cooking over a wood fire and stones behind the house as she and Yabu had done years earlier. Yabu was alive, but she had been moved to Makeni. I was told her mind had gone bad. I was unable to obtain more information of her status. The youth who had come up the hill to meet me was Yenki's twenty-five-year-old stepson. Yenki's welcome and recognition after thirty-six years was overwhelming. She must have forgotten that at least once I had cavalierly cut papaya fruit from one of their plants outside my back door years ago. No one ever confronted me or asked me what might have happened to the fruit. I do remember that it tasted wonderful.

My 1967–68 neighbor Yenki and her twenty-five-year-old stepson in 2004

I met other Binkolo people I had known who remembered me from long ago. I shared photos I had taken years earlier. The reception from them was very gratifying. I met the son of the fellow who had been my housekeeper, Foday the Hunter. Foday had died some years earlier.

~　~　~

When dependent upon local transport in West African travel one is subject to any number of variables and quickly learns to not be very demanding on the quality and safety of transport as long as a vehicle seems to be moving in the direction one wishes to go.

Seeking transport back to Makeni, Keh and I stood with Momoh Dura near Binkolo's only functioning water well. We watched a yellow Datsun van with two wooden benches and a canopy over its rear box approach us, coming down the road from Bumbuna. The four-cylinder pickup van lurched and sputtered as it neared us. I couldn't tell why it sputtered, either from faulty spark plugs or a poor gas line, but it was moving in the direction we wanted to go. We signaled to the driver. He stopped. As we negotiated our fare, the front passenger, a male, hopped out and graciously encouraged me to take his seat. I good-naturedly declined his offer, indicating that the man was older than me. Whether he was or not, he refused my offer. I took the front passenger seat—the "white man's seat." Keh and the earlier male passenger climbed onto the rear of the van, joining two other passengers—a woman and a child—and with the driver's cargo—six jugs.

My seating arrangements were not what one might expect. My legs were bent, my feet straddled an 8 cell battery abutting a 5-gallon plastic gasoline jug connected to the engine with a hose. The dashboard was cracked, shattered, broken, or missing in most places. Wires dangled from the dash console, hitting the driver's knees. At the top of every incline the driver disengaged the clutch. We coasted down each hill. We passed several charred, rusted frames of vehicles that had been attacked and abandoned during the war.

As we lurched to the crest of a small hill on the road it occurred to me that when we reached a police checkpoint near Makeni we would be stopped and the van would not pass inspection. There would be complications.

We approached a police checkpoint. I smugly pondered what would happen when we were stopped and what the "dash" would be to enable us to continue. I was wrong! The guard recognized the driver, the vehicle, or both. He strode to the barrier, a rubber or plastic rope strung across the road. He lowered it and waved us through. We slowed down, but did not stop. I was stunned!

A few yards later a large bang erupted from the back of the van. We stopped. The man who had given me his seat leaped from the back of the van and scurried away. I soon realized the explosion was not from something in the van but was simply a blown tire. The driver grabbed tools and began to jack up the van to change the tire. Both rear hubs had eight lug sockets, but only six lugs. The driver quickly replaced the tire, and we sputtered along. Arriving in Makeni, the driver did not enter the lorry park but simply stopped, let us out, and continued on his way. His cargo, palm wine or palm oil, may have been the reason we had no trouble at the police checkpoint. Binkolo is famous for the excellence of its palm wine. I drank some with Momoh Dura during my visit, and I hope to get back for more.

The next day Keh and I sought transport to Freetown. A FOSL couple from Montana was to accompany us back to Freetown. Both had been PCVs during and after my service, and they had shared the Buya Hotel with us. Returning to the lorry park, I approached John Kiester, Makeni's transport coordinator. John was the son of Pa Kiester, the Makeni merchant Dura and I had accompanied to the diamond mining area thirty-six years ago. Keh and I had visited John a couple of days earlier. During our earlier visit John was approached by a woman seeking a license or papers for a motorcycle. Keh thought the motorcycle had probably been smuggled into the country. There was no resolution of the matter while I was there, although Keh believed proper papers or a license would be available once some type of dash was given to John.

At the lorry park John approached a driver he knew and announced to him, "I have four white people going to Freetown." The white people were me, the Montana couple, and my guide, Keh. I told the driver we would be waiting at the Buya Hotel. Soon John and the driver came to the hotel. As we entered the van I asked John, "What is the fare?" He said, "Le10,000"—about $4 per person.

The driver was excellent; he avoided most of the road potholes. I believe he usually made two round trips daily between Makeni and Freetown. When we arrived in Freetown and exited the van, the driver charged each of us Le12,000. He said the increase was because we had luggage. This is a good example of what could start an ugly incident if someone, an expatriate or anyone else, begins to argue about the increased fare when in fact the increase is likely 50 cents or less. If a rider is mentally exhausted from living as a minority, is ill, is drunk, is ornery, or has other issues, one can get into a lot of trouble that could quickly get out of hand. However, if the rider has been in the country long enough to gradually understand some of the culture and will continue to be in the country, the rider can likely pay the driver the original cost and be done with it. It is in the rider's and the driver's best interest to maintain a relationship that reinforces a continued relationship. In the end both parties might chuckle over the disagreement, knowing that both parties have a relationship worth maintaining.

~   ~   ~

In Freetown I was later visited by Ismael Kanneh, the Makeni wood carver I had done business with. He came to Freetown to sell more carvings and gave me a gift of two others. I had known his father. Ismael found me at The Place Guest House and later crossed the street to have refreshments from an open bar before we parted. As we lounged Ismael suddenly stood up and disappeared. I thought he said, "I am going to eat." I purchased another beer for myself. Ismael soon returned. I was surprised to see him so soon and asked, "Ismael, where did you go?" He replied, "Patrick, I went to ease."

One of the patrons at the bar was a female school teacher who had fifty-two students in her classroom. Mindful that Freetown's water system was a source of *Salmonella* and that electricity was available only from private generators, I asked her, "Ma'am, how much longer will you put up with this nonsense?" Her response: "Sir, we have had a war here. Now we have peace. We can manage with difficulties over our water and electricity. This is much better."

She was right, but I am familiar enough with some of the country to at times be amused at some behavior and at other times be appalled at the level of chronic dysfunction, which can seem endemic, irresponsible, and appalling. For example, in May 2014 a member of the first Sierra Leone Peace Corps group (1961–63) sent three 40-foot containers full of medical supplies to Freetown. I was with this former PCV at the July 28–30, 2014, FOSL meeting held at Sapelo Island, Georgia. He has sent many shipments of medical supplies from Atlanta, Georgia, to Freetown. On August 11, 2014, even in the midst of the Ebola crisis, the supplies shipped in May had not yet been allowed into the country.

Later I was sitting on The Place's third-floor veranda. A Kenema diamond dealer and two of his friends approached me, wanting to make an arrangement of some sort about diamonds. I told them I had friends in the country. I told them I did not want to jeopardize my relationships and would be foolish to do so. They eventually left me, but their room was the one across the hall from mine. I still had considerable US cash in my money pouch. Knowing they were across the hall, I spent my last night in Freetown apprehensively wondering if they or someone else might try to break into my room.

16.

After Visiting in 2004

I returned to Minnesota and sent a letter to Keh to thank him for accompanying me during my visit. I used Dura's Freetown address. I received no response.

~   ~   ~

When I had visited Binkolo, four of the five village well water pumps were not functioning, having been damaged during the war. After I returned to the United States Chief Dura and I would periodically call each other on Saturday mornings. Early on I mentioned I would like to help him and the village fix the pumps. He said he wanted a water well on his compound; the cost would be $5,000. I couldn't afford to send that much money, but I eventually sold most of my wonderful jazz and R&B record collection and wired funds to him through an organization in Makeni.

The Chief phoned to thank me for the funds but encouraged me to never use that organization or that man again: "Don't use him again. He was very rude." During a later December Saturday morning phone call he mentioned the tropical rains and mudslides in Freetown.

He said it "has been raining dogs and cats." His language was still refreshing.

~ ~ ~

Alimamy Dura II, also known as Alimamy Dura Sesay II, died on February 23, 2007. After his death, Minnie, his Freetown wife, attempted to return to the United States but was unable to enter due to some type of visa problem. She may have overstayed her earlier visit. After the Chief's death his family sent me a compact disc video of the government and religious Binkolo funeral for him. Later the family informed and invited me to a ceremony marking the one-year anniversary of his passing but not in sufficient time for me to review the funeral video and try to use it as leverage to lobby my wife with the thought of returning to Binkolo for that ceremony. I eventually received the second video. Both are remarkable.

In 2009, his son Sanfa, who had been in the United States for about thirty-five years and worked as a probation officer for the state of Ohio, returned to Binkolo to seek to succeed his father as head of the chiefdom. Sanfa was elected to that position on December 27, 2009, succeeding his great-grandfather Umaru Gbokay, his grandfather P. C. Alimamy Dura I and his father, P. C. Alimamy Dura II. After the election Sanfa chose to be known as Paramount Chief Alimamy Dura III. During this time, prior to the election, one of the Sierra Leone newspapers referred to the family's ruling history as being for "donkey years"—a British phrase meaning a long time, referring to the length of a donkey's ears. Sanfa was a primary school student when I was in Binkolo in 1967–68.

During Sanfa's early leadership the chiefdom became involved in a Fambul Initiative Network for Equality program called Husbands School. The program was supported in part by the Impatient Optimist blog and the Bill and Melinda Gates Foundation. Before the 2014 Ebola outbreak a group of about fifty Binkolo fathers, men in their early twenties to their sixties, took a Husbands School class. When asked how many had beaten their wives, about two-thirds raised their hands. When asked how many would do it again, most of the same hands came up. When asked how many wanted to see their mother beaten, no one raised a hand. The men were then told that when they beat their wives they are beating their children's mother.

In 2013 the Aspen Institute gave Resolve 2013 Awards—a highly competitive, non-monetary award that celebrates progress made by governments toward delivering on the promise of universal access to reproductive health—to Kenya, Gambia, and Zambia and made special mention of Sierra Leone for "reducing the incidence of rape and gender-based violence" and raising awareness of related issues.

~ ~ ~

In December 2012 Momoh Dura, Alimamy Dura II's son, whom I had visited with in 2004, phoned and mentioned that he and others in Binkolo wanted to build a school in the village in my name. I later learned it would be a nursery school or kindergarten of some sort. I thought the idea of a nursery school was a fine one, but challenging, and I wondered who would staff it and how they might be paid.

In a country where primary school is free as long as a student has a school uniform, many teachers are not paid; sometimes they seek bribes to give students passing grades on a test. Some schools have "ghost teachers"—people on the school's teacher roster who are paid but do not teach. So much of the country can seem dysfunctional that the idea of a new school was daunting. The effects of the Ebola outbreak assaulted an entire generation of students.

In late 2013 Binkolo's Dura High School reopened. The 2014 Ebola outbreak made the earlier progress in all of the country impossible. According to the World Health Organization in April 2016, more than 14,124 Sierra Leoneans contracted Ebola, and 3,956 died. The number of deaths and orphans, the eight-month closing of schools in 2014 and 2015, and the banning of visibly pregnant primary and secondary students from school likely moved Momoh's original request in a different direction. The chiefdom made great efforts to address the Ebola issue when two persons with the virus returned to the area in 2014. In May 2016 Momoh told me that 285 people in the chiefdom developed Ebola and 99 of them died. Many were buried in the bush.

Shortly after that news I again heard that many young girls are now selling themselves to pay for school fees, food, and other necessities, with some of them as young as nine becoming pregnant.

The ten years of war, the Ebola, the closing of schools, the assault on the food system, and the persistent corruption had assaulted another generation. Chief Dura's 2004 phone comments to me have been reinforced again and again.

~   ~   ~

Chinese governments have a long involvement with the Sierra Leone people. During my 1966–1968 tour of service, the Formosan Chinese government had a number of agricultural demonstration farms in the country. One of them, staffed by three men, was in Safroko-Limba Chiefdom. Sierra Leone's relationship with Formosa ceased, and on July 20, 1971 Sierra Leone formally established diplomatic ties with the People's Republic of China (PRC). FOSL's 2004 annual meeting was held at China House, a meeting center in Freetown.

The PRC has made extensive investments in much of sub-Sarharan Africa, seeking minerals. In the case of Sierra Leone, contracts were signed to mine iron ore, bauxite, rutile, and other minerals. The PRC built, at no cost to Sierra Leone, a football pitch in the city of Bo, the capital of the Southern Province. At one time China offered to build, free, a bridge from Lungi to Freetown. What did China want in return? Access to all mineral rights under water in the Sierra Leone River Bay. The PRC has also submitted plans to build a new international airport closer to Freetown.

In February, March, and April 2015 a former PCV who served in Ghana, now a medical doctor, served with Doctors Without Borders in the Koidu area of Sierra Leone, working on the Ebola matters. He later told me that a local Sierra Leonean had commented that the British had been bad, the Americans not so bad, the Portuguese terrible, and the Chinese even worse. I later heard that during the 2015 Ramadan period some Chinese were telling their Muslim workers to avoid the fast so that they could keep working and not be weak during the day.

17.

Sketches

Culture Shocks

Culture shock can be the confused behavior or reaction of anyone who moves from one culture to another. Degrees of culture shock were common for many Peace Corps personnel once they entered their host country and when they returned home. It can be humorous, embarrassing, and harsh, but also very illuminating.

I saw effects of culture shock before I left Tanzania XIII training in 1966. One of our Swahili language teachers was a former PCV who had concluded his tour of service in East Africa a few months earlier. He may have been there too long, or had gotten too immersed or too isolated and returned to the US too quickly. He had a ghost-like, emotionally exhausted look in his eyes, and his face and body were pallid when he arrived in Syracuse that fall. To some of us he was a new hero. He had been to a place we did not yet know but where we thought we were to go. Whatever it was the man was experiencing in Syracuse, emotionally he seemed to be somewhere else. He knew Swahili, but he was still "out there." Some of us couldn't get enough of him.

After I returned to Minnesota to reconnect with my family for Christmas in 1968 I moved to Minneapolis in January 1969 and lived with former seminary classmates, all of us trying to sort out new futures. We had not been together very long when, after I used the bathroom, one of my former seminary classmates and now housemate reminded me: "We don't need to ration water here. It is OK to flush the toilet after urinating. It is the custom here."

~   ~   ~

With the availability of the Global Positioning System (GPS), cell phones, e-mail, Skype, the Internet, and other means of communication, it is difficult to begin to appreciate the degree of remoteness and isolation of some earlier PCVs. In my own case, when the rock and roll band the Doors released their self-titled album with the song "Light My Fire" in January 1968, I knew of the song but did not hear it until September. The Beatles' album *Sgt. Pepper's Lonely Hearts Club Band* was released on June 2, 1967, but I did not hear it until December 23—in the town of Moyamba when I was traveling to Shenge for Christmas.

~   ~   ~

Visiting a Sierra Leone vegetable garden and pulling up a pigweed plant. It is considered a weed in Minnesota fields but is a vegetable green in West Africa.

~   ~   ~

One of my first days in Freetown seeing an albino African man with a black African wife and children.

~   ~   ~

A new PCV school teacher moves into a very rural village far from Freetown. The new teacher is succeeding a rural development PCV who, in my mind, had a reputation for being a bit of a wild guy. A couple of days after moving in the new volunteer hears a knock on his door. A young woman greets the new volunteer and says, "Sir, I was the earlier volunteer's African wife. I will be your African wife too!" In

2014 I shared this brief snippet with the volunteer who allegedly had the African wife. He denied the story.

~   ~   ~

Visiting a remote Guinean village in the early 1960s, a white male PCV meets a local man who greets him with, "Bless me Father!"

~   ~   ~

During my term of PCV Sierra Leone service a very good college friend of mine sent me a copy of *Catch-22* by Joseph Heller. I had heard that Heller's book was a comedy of some sort. By the time I began reading the novel I had been in the country for more than a year, and my mind had begun to play tricks on me. My West African experience made it impossible for me to grasp any humor in the narrative. I read it as a straightforward story of a pilot in World War II. As I read it I kept thinking, "What's so funny about that?"

~   ~   ~

Most of the dogs in Sierra Leone I saw were thin, mangy, and full of fleas and worms. They were poor-looking creatures. An afflicted canine was adopted by a Peace Corps couple. The pup quickly became plump, and its skin recovered. Over time the dog developed some seemingly racist behaviors, particularly to anyone whose body language seemed more African than Western. Appropriately, the dog's owners named it Psycho. I do not recall the fate of Psycho after his PCV owners left the country.

~   ~   ~

Sometime during my second year of service my family sent me a photo of a bunch of people sitting around the steps of my family's Minnesota farmhouse. I looked at the photo and recognized everyone except one male. For a few days I thought the unknown person was a nearby neighbor of some sort. I eventually recognized the guy as one of my brothers.

~   ~   ~

Locked gas caps on all motorized vehicles.

~   ~   ~

Bare-breasted female dancers with the Sierra Leone Dance Troupe.

~   ~   ~

Bare-breasted women hauling water, pounding rice, cooking, washing clothes in streams, and working in farm fields.

~   ~   ~

Night watchmen armed with machetes sitting on the front or back porch of expatriate homes to protect against intruders.

~   ~   ~

One of my brothers married a woman from Malaysia whom he had met in Washington, DC. They moved to southern Minnesota near the end of the harvest season, in late September or early October. Seeing the now-empty harvested fields my new sister-in-law asked, "What are the farmers going to grow during the winter growing season?"

Ya Nancy

Nancy Kanu was my African mother. To me she was simply Ya Nancy. Like my American mother, I didn't ask for her—I just got her. Nancy was a stout, gap-toothed, warm, dark-haired, dark-skinned, smooth-faced woman who lived in a house near the American Wesleyan Mission compound on the north side of Binkolo. Even now I know I loved her.

She was a widow. She was a mother-in-law of Chief Dura. She seemed to like me and was very gracious to a bewildered young American. She told me she was my African mother. I took it as a matter of fact but was initially uncomfortable. I didn't know what she meant but decided it might be what she told any "porto"—white person—who might linger in the village. Whether she did that or not, I gradually knew something important had happened between us.

She had five children: sons Fred, Ned, and Hadric, and daughters Annie and Grace. Grace was a student at Binkolo's primary school. I have a memory, real or imagined, of her being impregnated by one of the primary school teachers. Annie was one of Chief Dura's wives who lived with him in the village. Ned and Fred were teachers at the teacher-training college in Magburka, a town not far from Makeni. I never knew what Hadric did for employment, but for some reason I was closer to him than to his brothers.

Ya Nancy invited me to spend the 1967 Christmas holidays with her family. I turned down the invitation and spent part of the holiday with three Tanzania XIII volunteers at Shenge, an oceanside posting two days from Binkolo by lorry. A few days after my stay in Shenge I went to a party in Freetown with Hadric and his friends as they were getting ready for the new year.

While I lived in the village Hadric became engaged to Esther, a Limba woman from another chiefdom headquarters up the road. I met Esther a couple of times and quickly could tell they were in love. Their joy and energy together was infectious. I was happy for them but also envious, having not yet felt the same emotions for a woman. I knew I wanted the same feelings sometime in the future. Hadric spoke to me about being the best man as their wedding. They married after I was evicted from the village and had left the country. From this distance I wish I had not been so anxious to leave the country and had been able to stay to witness the event. With Hadric, a brother-in-law of Chief Dura, it would have been quite the time. My life would have been even more enriched than it already had during the time I was in Sierra Leone. Later Hadric received a scholarship to study in the USSR, moved to Germany, and later died. I do not know if Esther managed to travel with him or not.

After my row with A. J. Sesay I returned to Binkolo only once before I left the country. I rode to the village in the small Series IIA Land Rover taxi owned and driven by Pa Bobo. Pa Bobo stopped his vehicle in front of the shop owned by the chubby, cheerful Muslim owner/farmer who lived across the road from where beef was butchered three times a week. I had purchased three chickens in Makeni. I got out of Pa Bobo's Land Rover, grabbed the chickens by their legs, and walked the quarter mile to Ya Nancy's home.

"I've come with a gift for you before I go back to America," I said as I came to the back stoop of her house. Nancy was slicing cassava leaf greens for an upcoming dinner. We exchange pleasantries. She was pleased and moved by my presence and the gift. I was moved and very emotional as I walked back to Pa Bobo and his taxi. I got into his vehicle and said, "Let's go." I was nearly sobbing, knowing that what I was a feeling was important, even if I did not know what it was. I didn't expect to hear from her again. I was really leaving the village and leaving the country.

~ ~ ~

After I returned to the US I wrote to her at a few times. She responded once, telling me of her trip to the United States, of Hadric and Esther having a baby girl, and of how much she enjoyed my visits to her house. She repeated that she had always regarded me as one of her sons.

Dear Pat,

I am really sorry for not replying to your letter ever since I received it. It is due to too much worries at home and especially my trip to America. On my arrival I met almost all my relatives dead, and so I had to go and attend to those burials. It is not my wish as to reply to your letters because I always regard you as my son. You really showed a kind spirit and friendliness to me.

I enjoyed the tour and your visits to me at my house. I wish you a find day and you will come again to see us. As for your question towards the marriage of Hadric, well!!! I am really happy that they have a fine baby girl with Esther but Hadric has got a scholarship for the USSR.

I hope you have settled in life and enjoying a nice job at home in which you always think of me. I will be very happy to see your picture with your house and home with your permanent address at the back.

Your memories live on deeply in me when all my children were all here for Christmas, I wish you were here. I am sorry to report to you that the Section Chief (Pa Bangura) of Mabamba where you used to go and work is seriously sick and that there are no hopes for his survival again.

All the children in this house wish you a happy and prosperous New Year and long life hopes of joy and prosperity.

Greetings to all at home in the States.

I am your African Mother, YA Nancy B. Kanu

~ ~ ~

Nancy's daughter Annie died of heart problems in 1974. Ned died in 2005. Fred was living in London in 2004. I was not able to learn of the status of her other children. At the 2009 Friends of Sierra Leone annual meeting in Minneapolis, one of the former PCVs who also knew Nancy mentioned that she was often visited by Siaka Stevens. I have no knowledge of the type of relationship they might have had. Ya Nancy died in 1994.

Soccer Match

My first exposure to soccer was during Peace Corps training in Syracuse. Twenty-two of us tried to play a game. Only two of the players had ever played the sport prior to coming to Syracuse. We were energetic, enthusiastic, and didn't know what we were doing.

I saw one soccer match during my stay in Binkolo. It was between the primary school teachers of Binkolo and Kamabai, the next good-sized village up the Kabala Road. Some of the players might not have been teachers but young men from each village—from the same tribe, since the inhabitants of both villages were primarily Limba. I didn't expect anything extraordinary at the match, but then it was to be the first soccer match I would ever watch. I was to be initiated.

The match was held on a level dirt clearing between the primary school buildings and two newer steel-framed structures whose construction had been started prior to my move into the village.

Spectators stood on the sidelines or sat on the ground; a few sat on two-legged, five-foot wooden benches from the school classrooms.

The game started. The ball was booted to one end of the field, booted to the other end, and then to the middle of the pitch. A melee of some sort between players quickly developed. Red laterite dust rose in the midst of the disturbance. Play stopped. Crowds rushed to the center of the pitch. Some of the wooden benches were carried from the sidelines and hurled into the crowd in the center of the pitch. The fighting eventually ceased. The chiefdom policeman summoned Chief Dura. The game was summarily canceled, after likely less than five minutes of play.

Years later, back in the United States I coached soccer for more than ten years, obtaining three licenses to do so.

You Are Invited

As I gradually began to understand some of the pattern of village life and became more and more accepted—or at least tolerated—there were times when I didn't feel like cooking a dinner for myself. On some of those occasions I would stroll down the hill to the main road and walk near a house inhabited by some people I eventually believed were chiefdom officials of some sort, possibly the Secretary or Treasurer; they were not farmers or traders of any sort. Sometimes a group of men would be sitting on the home's porch eating rice chop in the traditional African style of a large platter filled with rice and assorted sauces poured over it. All diners would dip one hand into the pile of food and wipe it into their mouths. I gradually picked up the technique well enough to not embarrass myself. Sometimes the man or woman who seemed to be in charge of the house would see me and say, "Mr. Patrick. You are invited" to come dine with us. I was not always successful in receiving a meal from them, but the times I did, it was very welcome. One time I mentioned to the woman in charge of the house, in what I thought was a simple comment, "Come and visit me some-time," with no specific intentions on my part—really thinking little of the invitation.

One day I was home reading in the heat of the dry season and I heard someone coming up the laterite foot path from the village. I heard "I am coming." It was the woman I had invited to visit me. She was wearing a very fashionable three-piece garment of largely purple garra cloth. The dress was a stunning example of high-end African clothing. I was not dressed fashionably, likely wearing cut-off white shorts and a tattered garra cloth shirt with a white, indigo, and brown–dyed diamond pattern. I wore that shirt so often that the yolk and back became so tattered that the shirt looked like it had been shredded. I was surprised by the visit and knew I had little of offer her. Not think-ing she would care for a beer, I may have offered a bottle of Vimto, the very sweet cola-like drink available at the shop down the hill. It was an awkward moment, with me not gracious enough to welcome her and begin to make small talk. It was likely an awkward moment for her without my ability to thank her for visiting me and asking what might be going on in her life. In the end I felt bad because I had some understanding of the effort she had made to dress in such fine clothing to respond to my invitation and because I was not capable of inquiring about anything of interest to her or to me.

Na Proper Bush Man

"Na Proper Bush Man" is a Krio expression describing a person
who has adjusted well the culture. For example, someone who carries
kola nuts to possibly share with someone walking or traveling
in the country, or who knows how to properly eat rice chop
with one's hand or how to drink palm wine.

His upper body was more than Apollonian—the most magnificent of the many I saw during my stay. He was beautiful in ways one might only dream about. His muscularity was the by-product of pumping leather bellows at a hearth fire where he heated wood and then iron to temperatures sufficient to pound and shape machetes and other hand tools for chiefdom farmers. His lower body was spindly, and inert from polio. He was a village blacksmith. He was a small man, but he was a giant!

His work area was a palm frond–covered four-post shelter near his dirt-sided palm frond–covered home. The tools of his trade were an anvil, leather bellows, hammers, iron tongs and pincers, firewood, and he himself. He moved through his workplace by pulling himself with his hands and elbows from here to there. He was quick, adroit, and a wonderful athlete. He was a self-sufficient man in a destitute farm village of less than forty people. The few times I saw him I enjoyed getting to know him. I wish I had been able to get to know him better.

He had two wives and at least one child. When I visited him, one wife tossed and fanned rice in a large, flat, rounded raffia disk. The rice would later be hulled by pounding in a wooden mortar with a long wooden pestle—hard and basic work.

His other wife might have been roasting peanuts in an iron bowl or pot for later grinding with a glass bottle. The peanuts would be mixed with beef or chicken for groundnut (peanut) stew. Or they might have been nursing a child or slicing okra, cassava, or potato leaf with rice and palm oil for a rice chop dinner late in the day.

The blacksmith was a true inspiration I will never forget.

Pa Bangura

Pa Bangura was Section Chief of Mabamba, a village a few miles from my home. He was delightful. When I visited Chief Dura in 2004 and mentioned Pa Bangura, he immediately mentioned Bangura had somehow been involved in the Boer War. If indeed that was the case, Bangura had to have been in his late seventies or eighties by the time I met him in 1968. He must have been a favorite of missionaries or the British when he was young to have been pulled out of wherever he had been years earlier. One could tell he had not always lived in a mud hut in a village far from anywhere.

I would walk out to visit him in the heat of the dry season. Most villagers would be working somewhere in the bush. Lying in his hammock on the porch of his thatch-roofed mud hut, Bangura would gently, and subtly, stroke his groin area under his garment as we chatted.

"Ah, Mr. Pat, Mr. Pat, those young girls, they are too much trouble!" I loved the man.

Bangura's trouble could have been an enlarged scrotum, not from sexual relations with women of any age but from drinking bad water. If he did, with clean water and basic antibiotics, his problem would have eased. Bangura died in 1974.

It can be easy to joke or chuckle about an issue one thinks one knows something about but actually does not understand at all. One time Saffie told me of a Freetown man whose penis was so large it extended to his knees, if not farther. Not believing it possible, I chuckled and responded that I thought she was exaggerating or something to that effect. In 2004 when I returned to Sierra Leone, I came across a mission group brochure that included photos of a man with a scrotum the size of a beach ball. I later learned that when surgery was done on the man's scrotum they discovered maggots inside. Another patient's penis was the size of a loaf of French bread before he had surgery.

Christmas 1967

Ya Nancy Kanu, my African mother, invited me to spend the Christmas holidays with her and her family in the village. I was honored but did not know how to respond. I did not know what I might have tried to give to her or any of her family. By then I had lived in the village about nine months and was probably still learning how live in Sierra Leone.

Instead, I, Dean Lonseth, and Dennis Cengel, two other Tanzania XIII community development volunteers arranged for a two-day lorry ride from Makeni to Shenge to spend Christmas with Darrel Leopold, another Tanzania XIII volunteer. Darrel lived in what I thought was an upscale brown mud-block house on a bluff overlooking the Atlantic Ocean. I thought it an idyllic and romantic site, believing it was a California-style home of some type. Shenge is not far from Plantain Island, two of many assembly places where Africans were gathered by slavers for slave ships bound for North America years earlier.

Our journey to Shenge included a one-night layover with Peace Corps and British Volunteer Service Organization volunteers who were stationed in Moyamba, where I heard the Beatles album *Sgt. Pepper's Lonely Hearts Club Band* for the first time. At a junction and lorry transport stop on the way there, we sat at a bar awaiting new transport, having one or more Star beers and some type of snacks, and I delighted in hearing recorded music by the Dark City Sisters from South Africa.

This trip involved riding in at least six vehicles. One of them was a huge lorry carrying large bags of palm oil kernels; two or three of us and our luggage rode in the back with the kernels. It was not a bus, but we got there. The road between Moyamba and Shenge was then a fairly good one. In 2014 the same road during the rainy season was in such rough shape that it was often impassible. Some of the bridges had fallen into so much disrepair that boards and tree trunks sometimes served as bridge decks.

Christmas Eve we dined on a fine meal, with Star beer, rice, fish, and vegetables cooked with peppers and palm oil. We later drifted into conversation and then sleep with the sound of ocean waves pounding the nearby beach.

That night Willis Conover, on the *Voice of America Jazz Hour*, broadcast parts of the Cannonball Adderley album *Mercy, Mercy, Mercy* at 8:15 PM in our time zone. The broadcast was repeated two hours later. We heard both broadcasts on our shortwave radio while each of us consumed more libations and any other items as we shared thoughts of Christmas in the United States with family and friends. Cengel and Lonseth became more and more maudlin as the effects of the food and beer became more and more pronounced.

Some of us recalled memories of seasonal collegiate football bowl games on the television or radio. Lonseth, late in the evening, yelled out something about the Slippery Rock University football team and, a bit later, deeper into his cups, loudly announced, "Patrick, this is horrible" as the later broadcast of Adderley's music ended. The radio was shut off, and those of us still awake drifted off into our slumber.

A day or two later I lorried into Freetown, where I partied with Hadric Kanu, Nancy's son, and his friends, and later with a group of PCVs. I don't recall kissing anyone that New Year's Eve. I was young, dumb, shy, and not prepared for any of the consequences.

House Warming

In the summer of 1968 a Sierra Leone Peace Corps Assistant Director and Northern Province Supervisor moved into a new house in Makeni. Some of us helped the supervisor lay tile on the home's cement floor.

When that task was completed the supervisor had a housewarming party for some of the people of Makeni and the local PCVs. Although he was an important person, he had been in the country for less time than some of the PCVs and wanted to make sure he did not miss inviting Makeni notables. So he asked a PCV who had been in Makeni much longer than him to put together a guest list and invite them to the party. The seasoned volunteer did as requested.

On the first night of the housewarming party, Friday, there was a very full house. A few hours into the festivities a Makeni police authority approached the PC supervisor and asked, "Do you know who is here?" The supervisor said something to the effect that he was not sure who had been invited. The officer told him, "There are some people here who should not be here."

The music was stopped. The lights were turned off. The house became silent as the police officer, flashlight in hand, went from person to person, face to face, identifying undesirables and escorting the uninvited or inappropriate to the door. One way or another many of us knew the police personnel, so we were not particularly worried about anyone he evicted. We remaining merrymakers quickly got going again and did serious partying until close to dawn Saturday morning.

Saturday afternoon and early evening many PCVs returned to the house to continue partying. By then some of the PCVs had been in the country almost two years and were traveling through Makeni on the way to Freetown to leave the county. Many were exhausted from their service and were not shy about seeking any edge of relief for their soon departure. That night a PC staff person ran out of cigarettes and asked a PCV school teacher for one. The PCV looked him over and suggested he "try a local one." The staff person did and eventually learned it was likely marijuana of some sort. Apparently it was the only time he had marijuana while in Sierra Leone.

We partied into the night again. Some returned to the house on Sunday to continue. I did not. I was spent from my hours partying and lorried back to Binkolo to begin to recover. It was quite the time.

Air Afrique

Years ago many Sierra Leone PCVs would holiday at Las Palmas, in the Canary Islands. Getting to Las Palmas often involved flying Air Afrique from Freetown and transferring in Dakar, Senegal. The flight between Freetown and Dakar might include short stops in Guinea, Guinea-Bissau, or Gambia. True or not, I heard of a Sierra Leone PCV who fell asleep on the flight to Dakar. Security was such that the passenger list was not closely checked in Dakar. The sleeping PCV was not disturbed and woke up when the plane landed in Paris. I suspect that somehow the PCV returned to Dakar and eventually to Las Palmas.

Sierra Leone Community in Minnesota

After my 2004 return to Minnesota I increased my contact with the Minnesota Sierra Leone community. The community holds an annual Independence Day celebration, and I was asked to be their keynote speaker at one of the events, each of which begins with a Christian prayer and a Muslim prayer. I began my speech by greeting the audience in the Sierra Leone languages I have some familiarity with: English, Krio, Limba, Mende, and Temne. I spoke for a few minutes, describing my association with the country as well as parts of the country I had been in. I finished my speech to silence. With my conclusion the woman who had invited me to speak rose and started to applaud. Gradually, and with her prompting, the audience gave me a standing ovation.

Postscript

I did not write this book by myself. People I knew long ago and have gradually reconnected with helped me to clarify issues, provided information and counsel, and updated me on a number of matters regarding what actually occurred during my time of service and what has occurred in recent years. I am particularly grateful to Gary Schulze, Alan Alemian, and Peter Andersen. Gary and Peter are former Sierra Leone PCVs, and Alan was my PC supervisor years ago. I am especially grateful to Peter for allowing me to use his photo of the Camel Back ("Takabla") rock formation near the village I once lived in.

~ ~ ~

The people and country of Sierra Leone, and the Peace Corps, were a gift to me. My relationship with P. C. Alimamy Dura II and his family was accidental, but it became profound with our intermittent contact over more than forty years. My 2004 return to the country and to Binkolo enabled me to gradually realize and understand that somehow I must have left a lot of myself there years ago.

I hope these stories and reflections give something worthwhile back to Sierra Leone and to other Peace Corps Volunteers. I hope some of these stories encourage readers to look at and learn about the world in slightly different ways.

To contact Patrick, write to him at

freebornfreetown@netzero.com

Made in the USA
Middletown, DE
25 September 2016